D0999051

WITHDRAWN FROM AVERY LIBRARY

WORKERS' PALACE
THE
SHIP
by Michel de Klerk

AVERYLC
NA
1153
.N55
W66
2013g

WITHDRAWN FROM AVERY LIBRARY

One of the logos designed by Michel de Klerk for Eigen Haard

WITHDRAWN FROM AVERY LIBRARY

FOREWORD

The year is 1909. In Pontanusstraat in Amsterdam-Oost, a group of spirited men gather together by candlelight. Deeply troubled by the abominable living conditions of workers in the city, they decide to set up an association to build good quality and affordable housing for the working classes. Eigen Haard is founded.

In its early years, Eigen Haard quickly made a name for itself with a unique building: The Ship. Michel de Klerk, architect and seminal figure in the Amsterdam School style of architecture, was commissioned to design a housing block in Zaanstraat containing over one hundred apartments and a post office. Dating from 1920, The Ship was to become his most famous building.

Evidently, the architect and the housing corporation were on good terms with one another, because De Klerk also created Eigen Haard's first official logo – an image of a man and a woman warming themselves by a fire. The flames of his design are still part of the current logo.

The Ship testifies to the fact that social housing can be both beautiful and comfortable. Never before had so much effort been put into the design of workers' housing. Each apartment has something unique about it, such as a special window or turret. Also, the apartments were far larger than what workers had until then been used to.

Eigen Haard owns a number of unique buildings, but The Ship is our treasure. It is included on a list of the world's 1000 most remarkable buildings of the 20th century. Besides being an icon of Amsterdam School architecture, it is a focal point of social housing. We therefore manage this building with great care. Up to the present day we allocate the apartments in The Ship to people on low incomes.

And we are committed to continue doing just this, now and in the future.

Nico Nieman
Chairman of the Board at Eigen Haard

Spire of The Ship, Op De Hoogte 1926

INTRODUCTION

The building known as Het Schip (The Ship) in the Amsterdam Spaarndammerbuurt neighbourhood marks the high point of social housing in the Netherlands. Here, workers were not only provided with good quality accommodation, but they were also given a beautiful home. Characterised by unusual brick bonds and richly decorated with works of art, The Ship was aptly described as a workers' palace. Even as early as the 1920's, architects from all over the world came to see the building and to this day it still attracts a great deal of interest. Since the beginning of the new millennium, The Ship houses a museum that informs visitors all about the Amsterdam School, the art and architecture movement to which the building belongs.

The architect behind The Ship is Michel de Klerk, sometimes referred to as the Rembrandt of architecture. De Klerk was an artist of many talents. To him, the exterior and the interior of a building were equally important. He toyed with shapes, not only as an architect but also as a draughtsman and furniture designer. In addition, his designs are typified by a distinctive brand of humour that, more often than not, requires time and a dip into architectural traditions to grasp. Viewing the work of Michel de Klerk and The Ship in particular, therefore makes for a pleasant exploration.
This book describes the visual language of The Ship and discusses the sources of inspiration that have led to the creation of this 'world wonder'.

Alice Roegholt
director Museum Het Schip

Michel de Klerk, circa 1909

CONTENTS

'Nothing is too good for the worker who has had to do without beauty for so very long.'

YOUTH AND ARTISTRY

Michel de Klerk was born into a large family on 24 November 1884. At the time of Michel's birth, his father *Joseph Leman de Klerk* was 78 years old and already had 24 children, 21 of whom were by his first wife Naatje van Moppes. On 30 November 1876 he married his first wife's niece *Rebekka Roeper*, who was 43 years his junior and thus younger than his eldest child. This second marriage resulted in four further children, Michel being the youngest.

Childhood in Amsterdam's Jewish Quarter

Michel de Klerk's parental home was located in the very poor Jewish quarter of Amsterdam, around Waterlooplein. Jewish residents who could afford to gradually moved away to new neighbourhoods such as the leafy Plantage, Sarphatipark and Weesperzijde areas, where grand new houses were being built. Meanwhile, the poor remained behind in the slum dwellings and mouldy basements of the old Jewish quarter, where diseases such as tuberculosis, cholera and malaria thrived.

The De Klerk family lived at Zwanenburgerwal 29, and it was here that Michel was born. Like many other Jews at the time, Joseph Leman worked in the diamond trade. For many years, this provided him with a steady income that enabled him to support his large family. However, the family circumstances changed when he died on 29 October 1886, just a few weeks before Michel's second birthday. The death of the family breadwinner meant that Michel's mother had to work as a washerwoman to make ends meet. During this period, the De Klerks moved house no fewer than eight times. It was fortunate that the family consisted of several older children who also worked to help put food on the table. With Michel's mother working, his sister Duif became like a second mother to the young boy and played an important role in his upbringing.

Although Michel de Klerk's first name and surname suggest otherwise, his family, like most of their neighbours, were of Jewish descent. They were High German (Ashkenazi) Jews and participated in all the major Jewish traditions. The surname De Klerk can be traced back to Michel's grandfather, who adopted it in 1811.

Accordingly, Michel de Klerk had a Jewish upbringing and at the age of thirteen he celebrated his Bar Mitzvah (the initiation ceremony when a boy reaches the age of 13 and is officially welcomed into the Jewish community). Being liberal minded, the young Michel was not very active in his faith and only occassionally went to synagogue. As Michel was not a Jewish name, people often called him by the Jewish name of Sam.

Little is known of Michel's childhood, but we do know that he went to primary school and this, it would seem, is where his genius first blossomed. The young Michel was constantly drawing and the story goes that when he had to stay behind after class one day, he secretly drew a picture of his teacher who sat quietly reading at his desk. When Michel's teacher saw the drawing he was so impressed that he put it up in the classroom. Architect *Eduard Cuypers* saw the drawing by chance and asked Michel to come and work at his practice. We do not know if this story is true. Another version claims that after primary school, Michel first went to work for his brother-in-law - a butcher - and then began taking drawing lessons from *Louis van der Tonge*. According to this version of events Cuypers supposedly spotted Michel's talent at Van der Tonge's.

Michel de Klerk as a young man

VIII Atelier voor architectuur

The studio of Eduard Cuypers, breeding ground of the Amsterdam School

Apprenticeship with Eduard Cuypers

The architectural practice of Eduard Cuypers was located at his place of residence at Jan Luykenstraat 2-4, straight across from the Rijksmuseum which had been built by his uncle *Pierre Cuypers*. Michel de Klerk was only thirteen years old when he started working at the practice as a young 'pencil sharpener'. His first commissions involved touching up sketch plans drawn by the architects who worked there. Later, he would also act as foreman for the office's building projects, including, for example, the construction of a sanatorium in Hoog-Laren in 1902 and 1903.

The Cuypers practice – or rather the studio – had a huge impact on Michel de Klerk's development. At the time, Eduard Cuypers was a renowned architect who designed a large number of buildings in the Netherlands, and later also in the Dutch East Indies (now Indonesia). He considered it essential that the architects working for him pursued a wide range of interests. To that end he allowed them access to his library and had a portfolio of magazines circulating among his staff. Cuypers also published a magazine of his own titled *Het Huis Oud & Nieuw* (The House, Old and New) devoted not only to the work of his studio but also to popular arts and crafts, ranging from carved wood art from the Dutch East Indies to hand-painted Delft pottery and Hindeloper chairs. In addition, it focused on Dutch architectural traditions such as the various types of wooden houses common in the nearby Zaanstreek region, some of which had a king post against the ridge beam of the roof. This king post was regarded as a link between heaven and earth.

It is clear that Michel de Klerk drew a good deal of inspiration from this magazine. Also, it is quite likely that he contributed illustrations, but we cannot be sure, since illustrations by members of Cuypers' own practice were always published anonymously.

Also working at the practice of Eduard Cuypers were the architects *Joan Melchior (Jo) van der Mey*, *Piet Kramer* and *Gerard Frederik la Croix,* who, along with Michel de Klerk, would initiate a new architectural movement: the Amsterdam School. For this reason the Cuypers studio is sometimes referred to as the breeding ground of the Amsterdam School. Although Cuypers was chiefly influenced by traditional styles and not overtly innovative himself, he offered his employees much opportunity and freedom to explore new creative directions. As a result, many of the architects who worked for him took part in the numerous competitions held in those days.

Evening Classes

In De Klerk's day, architectural studies as now offered by colleges and universities hardly existed. Any academic studies being taught would have been offered by the Royal Academy of Arts, the Royal Military Academy and the Polytechnic College Delft. Architects were first and foremost good draughtsmen. Most houses were built by contractors with architects rarely involved at all. Nevertheless, several courses were available where one could learn the building trade. For some time, De Klerk attended evening classes at the trade school *Industrieschool van de Maatschappij voor de Werkende Stand.* We know he stopped in 1906 but whether he actually completed the course remains a mystery. One thing is certain: during his time at the building engineering department of the Industrieschool he learned how to calculate constructions and was made familiar with the various architectural styles. The course was headed by *B.W. Wierink,* a fine artist and draughtsman who also illustrated books. Wierink taught Michel a great deal and encouraged him to further develop his drawing talents. From 1908 Michel started taking evening drawing classes at the Haarlem society *Kunst zij ons Doel,* where, working from models, he mastered the techniques of portrait and figure studies.

Michel de Klerk at the studio of Eduard Cuypers, circa 1900

Ex-libris for Lea de Klerk of the Jessurun family

Marriage to Lea Jessurun

Lea Jessurun, born on 16 June 1881, was a secretary working at the studio of Eduard Cuypers. She was of Portuguese-Jewish descent and possibly knew the De Klerk family already. In any case, Lea and Michel got to know each other well at the studio and judging by their letters, they were very close for a number of years. Michel called her Li and she, like many colleagues, addressed him as Sam. The couple were married on 31 March 1910 and were to have two children, Joost and Edo.

At this point in time, their Jewish faith did not play a very important part in their lives. It saddened Michel's mother in law, herself the daughter of a rabbi, that the couple just had a civil marriage ceremony. Nonetheless, De Klerk never turned his back on his Jewish identity, a fact demonstrated by a personalised ex-libris he once drew for his wife, depicting a woman under a weeping willow with a Hebrew text that read 'Lea de Klerk of the Jessurun family'.

Travels to England, Germany and Scandinavia

It was during his time at Eduard Cuypers' studio that Michel de Klerk became enthralled with new British architecture. In England, the Classical schemes that had long prevailed across Europe were being replaced by colourful brick houses with lush interiors and landscape gardens. As a direct response to the Industrial Revolution, *William Morris* and *John Ruskin* had started the Arts and Crafts Movement, which sought to restore beauty and craftmanship and championed art 'made by the people and for the people'.

Despite De Klerk's keen interest in this movement, his 1906 trip to London turned out to be a disappointment. All his attempts to find work failed and he found himself in a dirty big city with little perceptible evidence of the movement's ideals. In his letters to Lea he described the city as an 'ant's nest' with the British Museum as his only pleasure. The visit brought home to him that the modern British architecture he was looking for was not to be found in the city but in the countryside. Nevertheless, De Klerk continued to draw inspiration from the new British ideals of beauty and craftmanship, and residential house plans that he entered for competitions in 1907 and 1908 were clearly based on these ideals.

On two occassions, De Klerk also travelled to Germany. Among the places he visited was the medieval town of Rothenburg, where he developed an interest in its timber-framed houses and made several attractive drawings.

In 1908, the *Maatschappij tot bevordering der Bouwkunst* (Society for the Promotion of Architecture) organised a competition aimed at realising good quality homes for the working classes. The drawing submitted by De Klerk was titled 'Het Beloofde land' (The Promised Land) and clearly demonstrates the importance he attached to colour use.

At the beginning of 1910, De Klerk spent a short time working as foreman in Belgium where the practice of Eduard Cuypers had been

Drawing of Stockholm harbour by Michel de Klerk, 1910/1911

Competition entry Het Beloofde land, 1908

commissioned to construct an exhibition pavilion for the Brussels World's Fair. It was to be his last contribution to the Cuypers practice because after marrying Lea, the newly weds left the studio and travelled to Denmark and Sweden. This extended honeymoon turned out to be of great significance because it was in these Scandinavian countries that De Klerk came across a completely new style of romantic architecture. During the trip he made numerous travel sketches and studies of buildings, furniture and arts and crafts. In Sweden he visited the Skansen Open-Air Museum and captured several of its buildings in drawings, but one of the highlights of the trip was the Paladshotel in Copenhagen, by architect A. Rosen. De Klerk's sketches of the hotel spire are believed to have inspired him later on when designing the spire of The Ship.

It is unclear how the couple could afford the trip but they probably had some money saved up from their time working for Cuypers. Also, Lea's family was quite well off and possibly provided some financial support. In addition, Michel continued to work during the trip. While in Stockholm, for example, he sent in a drawing for a competition to design a funeral chapel at a graveyard, which he titled 'Reincarnation'.

Working for Architect Baanders

After their return to the Netherlands at the beginning of February 1911, Michel and Lea first took lodgings in Andreas Bonnstraat. In October they moved to Jacob Marisstraat 24 (at that time still part of the municipality of Sloten), where they lived until May 1917, when they settled at Lomanstraat 26.

De Klerk was soon offered a job as foreman/draughtsman with *Herman Baanders*, who had taken over his father's architects practice and expanded it further with the assistance of his brother *Jan*. De Klerk knew Jan Baanders well from the time they had both trained as architectural draughtsmen at the *Industrieschool*.

The Baanders practice was located at Herengracht 495, the top floor of which housed the studio of painter *Lizzy Ansingh*, with whom Herman had close ties. The address also accommodated *Nederlandsche Grondbriefbank NV*, a real estate investment bank that had been set up by Herman Baanders and his brother-in-law. This 'Grondbriefjesbank' made it possible for the practice to develop its own building projects. De Klerk performed a wide range of tasks for the Baanders practice, including the design and building supervision of an Old Dutch style pavilion for an exhibition in Berlin. He also collaborated on the restoration of the Waalse Church in Amsterdam and on a house designed by Jan Baanders in the Van Miereveldstraat. Not long after, De Klerk stopped working for Baanders and established himself as an independent 'architectural draughtsman'.

De Klerk remained good friends with the Baanders brothers, who even allowed him the continued use of his workplace at Herengracht as well as the practice's facilities. He once made an impressive painting of Jan Baanders, portraying him as a bohemian with a cigarette in his mouth. De Klerk was also friends with Jan's sister *Tine Baanders* – a well-known Dutch illustrator of books – and her good friend sculptor *Louise Beijerman*. Letters sent to Tine by De Klerk

Michel de Klerk

Michel de Klerk with architect Jan Baanders

Water monument in Venlo, designed by Michel de Klerk

reveal that he was very fond of both her and Louise and in one of his letters he writes Tine that he had gone rowing with Louise. He also designed an ex-libris for Louise which showed a woman tolling bells, a humorous reference to her surname 'Beijerman' (man who tolls bells). In 1921, they worked together in Venlo to create a water monument in Wilhelminapark honouring the departure of the 80-year old mayor *H.B.J. van Rijn*. In line with De Klerk's sense of humour, the work is a tomb with two frogs sitting on top of it under an umbrella. It is not known how he came to be commissioned for this project, but Mayor Van Rijn was a great instigator of social housing in Venlo so it is possible that he had contacts with De Klerk. Another explanation is that Louise was commissioned and that she in turn asked De Klerk to work with her on the project. In any case, De Klerk's friendship with the Baanders family often helped him to get commissions.

Draughtsman

In 1913, the first Dutch shipping exhibition *ENTOS (Eerste Nederlandsche Tentoonstelling Op Scheepvaartgebied)* was held in Amsterdam-Noord and De Klerk took part in a competition to design a poster for the event. His entry was a highly detailed drawing of sailing ship *De Zeven Provinciën*, a scale model of which was on display at the Rijksmuseum. It won him second prize. In a competition to design a poster for The Hague Tourist Board he was awarded first prize. De Klerk's drawing talent proved a useful source of extra money to supplement his architect's income. In 1921 he designed the cover of the book *Grenzen* by novelist *E. d'Oliveira*. As we have come to expect from De Klerk, the result is intriguing and finely detailed; a man with a Javanese head cover and a black cat on his shoulder holds a flickering candle, while a sinister palace looms in the background. The book presumably sold well, since one edition states on its flyleaf that 'Mr. M. De Klerk' wishes to make it known that 'the letters B.N.A. [Royal Institute of Dutch Architects] placed behind his name are based on a misconception'.

De Klerk also made a large number of portraits, mostly as a hobby and occassionally to make some extra money. Besides making portraits of his wife he immortalized countless friends and acquaintances, including the revolutionary Dutch poetess *Henriëtte Roland Holst*. Like many artists of his time, De Klerk's political views were left-wing oriented. He enjoyed going to see Henriëtte at Oude Buissche Heide and drew her portrait during a visit in 1921, portraying her as the stern and serious woman she could sometimes be. Her husband *Richard Roland Holst* - a well-known artist who made many portraits himself - wrote an extensive article expressing his amazement at De Klerk's portrait art. He remarked that unlike most artists, Michel de Klerk did not begin to draw according to a preconceived scheme. Instead, he first allowed himself to take in the model, whereupon he analised the shapes. As in his architecture, this brought on a play of shapes in which he aimed for a high degree of perfection.

Cover illustration by Michel de Klerk for the novel Grenzen

Portrait of poetess Henriëtte Roland Holst by Michel de Klerk, circa 1921

Poster design by Michel de Klerk for the ENTOS exhibition, 1913

Furniture Designer

Apart from his work as an artist, draughtsman and architect, Michel de Klerk also designed furniture. His creations include a wide range of pieces, including chairs, tables, lamps, clocks and heating stoves. For his own bedroom he designed a large wardrobe featuring wood carving that to some extent refers to the Dutch East Indies. At the end of 1912, the Amsterdam solicitor *J.H. Polenaar* gave him one of his first real assignments, namely, to design him a suite of bedroom furniture. The finished pieces made such an impression on Polenaar's brother-in-law *F.J. Zeegers* – who was the director of furniture firm *'t Woonhuys* – that he asked De Klerk to come and work for him. Due to the slackened building trade, De Klerk was only too happy to accept this job proposal. At 't Woonhuys, he was given his very own showroom to display his furniture pieces. He also designed the panelling of the room himself. De Klerk's furniture suites were far too daring, elaborate and detailed to be mass produced. According to a magazine writing about his furniture, De Klerk put his heart and soul into his pieces. Once again, he drew inspiration from a wide variety

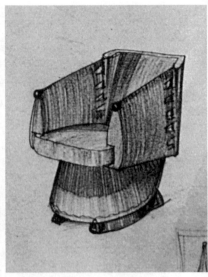

Sleigh chair by Michel de Klerk   Design for 't Woonhuys, 1916

of sources; his celebrated chairs, for example, are clearly related
to the sleighs and farmhouse chairs he had seen during his travels
in Scandinavia.

The production of De Klerk's furniture pieces required a great deal
of handiwork and they were made from costly varieties of wood.
Consequently, the pieces were expensive to produce and thus only
affordable to the well off. In trade magazine *Architectura*, Michel de
Klerk expressed his gratitude to 't Woonhuys for selling his designs,
in spite of the fact that the average clientele disapproved of such
'unsaleable models'.

Among the buyers of his furniture suites were a certain Mr. and
Mrs. *Dutilh*, a couple who were married in May 1918 and needed a
dining room suite for their newly rented house on Keizersgracht.
At furniture firm 't Woonhuys, which was located on one of the
corners of Leidsestraat, they saw De Klerk's furniture suite which,
although 'daringly modern', they took a great liking to. The sideboard
bulged outwards and had stained glass closing it off at the front.
Accompanying the dining table, which was round rather than square,
were two bizarre chairs with leather armrests as well as four chairs
without armrests. Each chair was upholstered in green 'velours
d' Utrecht' (Utrecht velvet) and richly sculpted in mahogany and
ebony. Unable to resist temptation, the Dutilhs decided to purchase
the suite. While not buying De Klerk's panelling, they did add to their
purchase the purple and green rug on which the furniture suite was
displayed, which was equally 'bizarre in design and colour'. In spite of
doubts as to whether they would continue to like the furniture, the
couple never regretted the purchase and the suite went with them
every time they moved house.

Reception room designed by Michel de Klerk, 1916

Dining room chairs for 't Woonhuys, designed by Michel de Klerk, 1915

Wendingen Magazine

Michel de Klerk was an individualist for whom self-expression was paramount. The idea of a big practice with a large number of permanent staff members did not appeal to him. Although he was occasionally forced to call in the help of others, he preferred to keep this to an absolute minimum.

Even so, he was a collegial man. As a member of the Amsterdam society *Architectura et Amicitia*, he would from time to time take part in discussions about art and architecture. On these occasions his personal views and ideals concerning the role of architecture made him stand out.

As a matter of course, De Klerk was asked to join the editorial staff of the famous magazine *Wendingen*, which was published by Architectura et Amicitia under the direction of architect H. *Th. Wijdeveld*, also an initiator of the Amsterdam School. De Klerk declined, but made regular contributions to the magazine, which was founded in 1918 and had its last issue in 1931. Several issues of Wendingen – which roughly translates as 'upheaval' or 'inversions' – also appeared in English, French and German. With its distinctive square format and raffia binding, Wendingen focussed on the various facets that inspired the Amsterdam School. Particularly notable editions include those on shells and crystals, because as Wijdeveld once said, 'what are we architects when compared to a shell or crystal, nothing whatsoever'.

Wendingen, Public housing issue May 1920. The cover is by Michel de Klerk

Wendingen with furniture and interiors by Michel de Klerk, no. 7-10, 1925

Wendingen with completed buildings by Michel de Klerk, no. 9-10, 1924

Wendingen with completed buildings by Michel de Klerk, no. 9-10, 1924

Wendingen, East-Asian Art issue, no. 4-3, 1921. The cover design is by De Klerk

De Klerk was in any case closely involved in the issue about social housing. Apart from being a member of the editorial team for this issue, he designed the cover, which had a nest of birds on the front and a beehive on the back. He also designed the covers for two other issues of Wendingen: the second issue dating from February 1918 (which had a picture of one of his clock designs inside) and a 1921 issue about East Asian art.

February 1919 saw the publication of an issue of Wendingen almost exclusively devoted to buildings designed by Michel de Klerk. In an accompanying text, the architect *K.P.C. de Bazel* wrote in laudatory terms of De Klerk's work: "De Klerk shows he is one of the very few with the talent to breathe soul into brick and make it come alive". The issue contained 22 pictures and eight plans of De Klerk's buildings, including many drawings of the as yet unfinished building The Ship. After De Klerk's death, his work continued to be featured regularly in Wendingen, with an issue featuring travel sketches he had made in places such as Loosdrecht and in Scandinavia, an issue focusing on the portraits he had made and one about his furniture and interior design. There was even a special issue about De Klerk's unrealised architectural projects, such as the designs he submitted for competitions. It was clear that Michel de Klerk was a source of great inspiration to many other architects. Wijdeveld described him as 'a prophet' who knew how to shape the city into a unit and laid an innovative foundation for architectural forms: "He drew with urgency and lust, out of duty and as recreation. He was at once the most childish and the most powerful of us all and he played with shapes in the unfettered realm of his fantasy. He reached where others saw nothing, acted where others merely thought and was so ardent in his desire to give, that when denied the opportunity to express his architectural spirit on a large scale, he fulfilled this urge in one street, doing so in a manner that could have served an entire city".

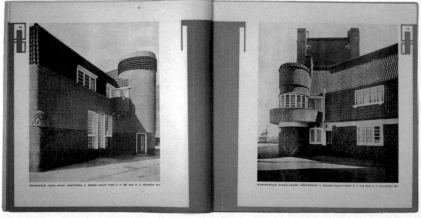

The Ship in Wendingen, 1924

AMSTERDAM SCHOOL ARCHITECTURE

Michel de Klerk took a critical view of the architectural vision of the architect *Hendrik Petrus Berlage*, who was widely admired at the time. In the 1916 edition of *Bouwkundig Weekblad* (Architectural Weekly) marking Berlage's 60th birthday, De Klerk reproached Berlage for leaving insufficient room for the architect's individual creativity. "After several years of seeing the Berlage style, I wondered if the *art* of architecture would ever return", De Klerk wrote. While acknowledging his major contribution to the building trade, De Klerk felt that Berlage "never quite got round to the art of architecture". As De Klerk saw it, Berlage did not fully grasp "the exhilaratingly new, sensationally shocking and impressively imposing" possibilities of the time.

Nevertheless, he conceded that Berlage had purified the building trade and that his new Stock Exchange, his office buildings for insurance company *De Nederlanden* and the villa *Parkwijk* had set a trend. Just like De Klerk, Berlage had a love of traditional craftsmanship and in his buildings he collaborated with a multitude of artists, including Richard Roland Holst. On this point however, De Klerk felt that Berlage was distressingly limited, being "too exclusively technical and utilitarian". As an architect, De Klerk wanted to go much further; he believed architecture should be about the art of building. While the sculptural art on Berlage's buildings served an exclusively decorative purpose, De Klerk integrally incorporated it into the accentuation of his buildings.

Amsterdam School

With his views on modern architecture, Michel De Klerk soon became the leading figure of a new architectural movement that had ideals of expressionistic and utopian beauty as its guiding principles. The movement's views corresponded to those of the popular Dutch

Design for a funeral chapel by Michel de Klerk, circa 1910

literary group *De Tachtigers* and coincided with the gradually growing appreciation of the colourful paintings of the Dutch painter *Vincent van Gogh*. But while art forms such as literature and painting allow unlimited expression, architecture is restricted by technical and social requirements. De Klerk's work came forth from a personal quest for greater beauty for society as a whole. The fact that he had the ability to actually realise his ideals makes his work even more special.

Work by De Klerk and by contemporaries with whom he had worked closely at the practices of Eduard Cuypers and Baanders was amply represented at an exhibition held in 1915 at the Stedelijk Museum in Amsterdam to mark the 60th anniversary of the architectural society Architectura et Amicitia. De Klerk's designs, which were on display in the Hall of Honour alongside work by Berlage, included sketch plans for social housing as well as two designs that were never realised: the funeral chapel he designed while in Sweden and a water tower of reinforced concrete.

At this stage, the new architectural movement was not yet known as the *Amsterdam School*. It was architect *Jan Gratama* who first coined the term in his contribution for the monograph published on the occasion of Berlage's 60th birthday in 1916. Gratama described the architects of the new movement as "having grown up with Berlage's principles but now desiring the blossoms of the tree, of which the trunk and branches represent rationalism. Within the conventional, rational style they aspire to a lively, sensitive, profoundly personal beauty".

It was not long before the movement gained a firm footing and 'Amsterdam School' became a term of endearment. From 1920 onwards, elements of the Amsterdam School style were to be found in almost everything being designed or built in Amsterdam. In 1918, at the recommendation of Architectura et Amicitia, Michel De

43 Klerk joined a commission of the *Nationale Woningraad* (national housing council) which was drawing up a list of architects for Dutch housing corporations to use. One of his fellow commission members representing the *Nederlandse Bond van Architecten* (Royal Institute of Dutch Architects) was architect K.P.C. de Bazel, with whom De Klerk was on friendly terms. In the 15 December 1923 issue of the magazine for *Volkshuisvesting en Stedebouw* (public housing and town planning), a representative of the *Nationale Woningraad* described the working method of the two architects. De Bazel was 'more immediate in his recommendations' while De Klerk was 'seemingly more hesitant and seemingly softer, yet in actuality not less resolute'.

De Klerk was much admired by the other Amsterdam School architects, who were particularly impressed with his imposing drawing for the 1917 competition to design a new *Rijksacademie van Beeldende Kunsten* (National Academy of Fine Arts) in Amsterdam. The competition attracted entries from 110 architects and De Klerk won second prize, but many of his colleagues disagreed with the jury's decision and felt that De Klerk's design was superior and deserved to win. During an evening meeting by Architectura et Amicitia he was even spontaneously crowned with a laurel wreath, an event that his architect friend Piet Kramer would later describe as the first public acknowledgement of his genius. Further criticism of the jury's decision came from engineer *A. Boeken*, who wrote in *Elsevier's Geïllustreerd Maandschrift* (Elsevier's Illustrated Monthly) that De Klerk's design formed a majestic and unified whole that was more appealing than the winning plan by architects *B. Bijvoet* and *J. Duiker*. Boeken did not understand how the building could be criticised for being too decorative: 'Then one would also have to criticise the wondrously marked orchid for lacking the natural regularity and colour simplicity of the buttercup'.

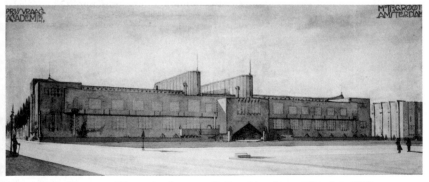

Michel de Klerk's competition entry for a new National Academy of Fine Arts, 1917

Despite being lavished with praise, De Klerk always remained a modest, somewhat shy man. His son Joost later recounted how they once received an unexpected visit from the British *Architectural Association (AA)* secretary *F.R. Yerbury*, who rang the doorbell and asked De Klerk, who opened the door in his dressing gown, if his master was at home. In his work, however, De Klerk was passionate and highly driven. Whenever he had a commission he would become completely immersed in the project at hand and have little time for anything else. Also, he worked with meticulous precision, something he may have inherited from his diamond cutting father.

Architect-Artists

The period of the Amsterdam School stretched from 1910 until around 1935, but its architects never constituted a well-organised movement with a clearly defined set of objectives. When Gratama observed that a certain Amsterdam School group had taken a radically new architectural direction it concerned a name only and not a fixed mission. Generally speaking, the term Amsterdam School covers architecture that features an artistic use of materials such as bricks and roof tiles and where the total composition of the facade forms a unified whole. Rebelling against straight lines and rigidly implemented systems, the movement was expressionistic and represented beauty, imagination and romance.

Michel de Klerk, Piet Kramer and Jo van der Mey were the three main figures of the Amsterdam School. They made one another's acquaintance at the practice of Eduard Cuypers and mutually aspired to transform the act of building into an art form. Although initially good friends, the three architects fell out during the construction of the Scheepvaarthuis (Shipping House) in 1915. Their views were typified by a strong appreciation of traditional materials coupled

The studio of Eduard Cuypers (Michel de Klerk third from right), circa 1906

with the use of modern building methods. They regarded art as an essential element of architecture, regardless of whether it involved a minute building detail or a dominant expressive form.

Architecture was seen as a form of public space art and the building process was about designing the spatial surroundings. The colour of the bricks, the expressive extensions, the shapes of windows, the arrangement of the glazing bars within windows, small sculptures on the facade; all were equally essential in the composition of the larger work of art.

In the first issue of Wendingen dated January 1918, architect H. Th. Wijdeveld wrote about the new movement in the following terms: 'Besides architecture in its new composition of pure structure, there is a recognition of the glorious appearance of the Imaginatively minded, who play naively with the treasures of rationalism. In this ambience, rigid masses of wall are transformed into pliant architectural expressiveness and in playful motion the cadence of spatial development follows'. Wijdeveld compared Michel de Klerk to the famous German dancer *Gertrud Leistikow*: 'the exaltation of beauty grows from their individualism … and then considerations fall silent and we may only admire'.

Spread

Buildings designed in the style of the Amsterdam School can be found far beyond the boundaries of Amsterdam. The designation 'Amsterdam' merely derives from Gratama's observation of the new direction taken by a group of Amsterdam-based architects during the period 1910-1915.

Accordingly, the abundance of Amsterdam School architecture in the capital city has less to do with the style's geographical origin than it does with the fact that it became the dominant style of social housing. This was made possible chiefly through the efforts of Floor Wibaut, who became alderman for housing in 1914, and his brother-in-law Arie Keppler, who was appointed the first director of the municipal housing service in 1915. Both were committed to providing working class people with good quality and beautiful houses. From 1915 onwards, the Amsterdam School style flourished under the recommendations of the *Schoonheidscommissie* (municipal committee on beauty), whose members passed an aesthetic judgement on newly planned buildings. Also favouring the Amsterdam School style were most of the members of the committees making plans for expansion in Plan Zuid and Plan West. In this way, a substantial share of Amsterdam's new residential neighbourhoods came to have a distinct Amsterdam School appearance.

Amsterdam School architecture can be found almost anywhere in the Netherlands, from a cow shed in Roosendaal to a church in Friesland. The northern region of Groningen is even quite famous for its multitude of Amsterdam School buildings. Villas built in Amsterdam School style can be found throughout the country. Notable examples include the magnificent country house *'t Reigersnest* in Oostvoorne by the architects *P. Vorkink* and *Jac. Ph. Wormser*, and the *Park Meerwijk* villas in Bergen by five Amsterdam School architects. Tile manufacturer Heystee commissioned architect *Frits Staal* for the

The 'cigar' at the corner of Zaanstraat and Hembrugstraat, circa 1925

villa project, who in turn called in the help of four colleagues to help him design the villas: his later wife *Margaret Kropholler*, *Piet Kramer*, *Gerard Frederik la Croix* and *Cornelis Jouke Blaauw*. The finished buildings represent the huge richness and artistic freedom of the Amsterdam School.

De Klerk, Inspirer of a New Movement
Michel de Klerk saw it as his duty to inspire craftsmanship and once again elevate it to an art form. While the applied arts comprised of individual arts and crafts, architecture united them all in a single entity. To the Amsterdam School architects, it went without saying that their buildings were an all-embracing total work of art, or Gesamtkunstwerk. Architecture did not, however, merely play host to other forms of craftmanship; the architects in their turn also created designs for applied arts and graphics.
De Klerk knew how to merge craftsmanship with modern building methods, effortlessly combining a concrete construction with facade ornamentations of typically Dutch traditional materials such as common 'Dutch' bricks and roof tiles. He understood that masonry was craftmanship and that brick bonds enhanced and beautified a building. Colour and structure were hugely important to him and he exercised great care in the composition of mortar and in his choice of brick and roof tile.
Various types of brick bond patterns can be found in De Klerk's buildings. Sometimes he used vertically laid bricks, as in the vertical cylinders in the stairwells of his first housing block at Spaarndammerplantsoen. For expressive curves De Klerk often used header bonds, a brickwork pattern consisting entirely of headers displaced by half in each row. In this way the curve could reach its full potential without requiring horizontal or vertical lineation.

Apart from bricks, De Klerk incorporated materials such as wood and wrought iron into his buildings. His second housing block at Spaarndammerplantsoen, for example, is decorated with an 'old-fashioned' wood clad bay window. A striking detail is that the planks were clad vertically and therefore do not fulfill their original purpose of preventing water from entering through chinks. Wood was extensively used for the windows, which often have horizontal bars and are thus known as 'ladder windows'. Also, De Klerk did not limit himself to traditional glazing bars but sometimes gave windows deviating shapes that were better suited to the total composition. Elevating traditionally crafted materials to a higher level is just one aspect of De Klerk's work. His building materials were the tools of his craft, but the work of art is ultimately made by the artist and not by his tools. To De Klerk, architecture was public space art and everything revolved around the composition as a whole. As *P.H. Endt* expressed it in the seventh issue of Wendingen in 1918, 'For De Klerk, a building is always the materialisation, the approach in building materials, of a presupposed total picture. His scheme is made up of the contrast between vast surfaces and small, finely detailed chunks, which he turns into a 'day out'.

The total compositions designed by De Klerk were inextricably related to their spatial context. At Spaarndammerplantsoen, the facades of the two blocks facing the public green have strongly accentuated stairwells giving the buildings an air of stateliness and grandour: a fine example of composition and spatial surroundings strengthening one another.

Doorway of The Ship at Zaanstraat, circa 1923

Architectural Development

The stairwells in the first and second block at Spaarndammer-plantsoen are particularly interesting in that they lend a unique character to the spatial composition of the facades. Protruding slightly from the facade, the stairwells of both blocks have vertical cylindrical forms that were in turn carried out in a vertical brickwork pattern. This is an example of smaller details strengthening the total work. Although they form part of a larger composition, the stairwells simultaneously form powerful independent sub-components, executed in ever smaller details.

The last buildings designed by De Klerk (Dageraad and Vrijheidslaan) show fewer of such sub-components. Also, there is less detailing and a greater emphasis on the cadence of the main composition.

The third block at Spaarndammerplantsoen known as The Ship has 'the best of both worlds' in that it marks a transition from finely executed detail to a purified total composition. What makes this building so spectacular is the manner in which the detailing relates to the main composition. Attracting admirers ever since its completion, The Ship not only stands out as the highlight of De Klerk's architectural career, but also forms the highlight of the Amsterdam School style as a whole.

Uithoorn

The first implemented design for a residential property by De Klerk was a small house in Uithoorn. His design was relatively straightforward, distinguished chiefly by a recessed corner and the use of the elegant 'Monk bond' brick pattern, consisting of two stretchers to one header in each course. However, it was only partially carried out, the brick bond being discarded and the house ending up a lower height than originally intended. Perhaps the building plan was just too innovative to be realised in its entirety.

Michel de Klerk's design for a house in Uithoorn set an example in its use of brick bonds

Hillehuis was Michel de Klerk's first major assignment

Nevertheless the design proved very influential, being published in 1916 in the *Handboek Burgerlijke Bouwkunde* (handbook of civil architecture) by *L. Zwiers* and *J.P. Mieras* and named as an example of the interesting possibilities of brick bonds. In the years that followed, a large number of Amsterdam School architects, including De Klerk himself, would make use of this brick bond. Several other elements, such as the broad half-round rain gutters with the pointed ends, would also make a reappearance in later works.

Hillehuis

De Klerk's first major project was to design the Hillehuis at Johannes Vermeerplein in the Museumplein neighbourhood. Building contractor *Klaas Hille* and his partner *G. Kamphuys* initially approached the Baanders practice, but when De Klerk (who worked there as draughtsman) came up with an innovative design, the Baanders brothers decided to pass the project over to him. What made the Hillehuis design so groundbreaking was that the building's facade was interpreted as a whole with the floor plans of the interior barely visible from the outside. It was no longer about individual houses but about the total work. De Klerk played with shapes and ornamentation, as can be seen in the detailed doors and chimneys and in the various forms of brickwork ornamentation. Hillehuis, as the building came to be called, was in fact the beginning of what would become the Amsterdam School style of architecture. It established De Klerk's name as an architect and earned him many other commissions.

Shipping House at Prins Hendrikkade, circa 1920

Shipping House

When architect Van der Mey was commissioned to build the
Scheepvaarthuis (Shipping House) in 1912, he asked his friends Michel
de Klerk and Piet Kramer, whom he knew from the Eduard Cuypers
practice, to assist him. Ever since the opening of the North Sea Canal
in 1876, Amsterdam's shipping companies had been prospering, and
they now required a joint office. Their new headquarters were to be
symbolically located where the ships of the Dutch East India Company
(VOC) once left on their long voyages, right in the centre of the city.
The building was to exude the kind of grandeur that passengers might
expect if they were to set out on a long sea journey. Money was no
object and the 'crème de la crème' of Dutch artists were invited to
make a contribution. Javanese artists specialised in wood carving
even came all the way from the Dutch East Indies to work on the
building.

With the three architects collaborating so closely, it is not always
clear who designed which part of the facade. Formally speaking,
Van der Mey was responsible for the exterior but it is likely that
Michel de Klerk and Piet Kramer had an important influence on the
end result. A great deal of the sculptural work on the building is by
Hildo Krop – who would soon be appointed as official city sculptor
– as well as *Willem Brouwer* and *Hendrik van den Eijnde*. Krop
later stated how Michel de Klerk gave him directions concerning
the appearance of his sculptures. Also, drawings by De Klerk of
sculptures for the Shipping House show similarities to sculptural work
at Spaarndammerplantsoen. The interior of the boardroom of the
Netherlands Steamship Company on the second floor of the Shipping
House was designed by Michel de Klerk and Piet Kramer, while De
Klerk was solely responsible for the interior of the boardroom of the
Royal Packet Navigation Company (KPM) on the third floor. Here De
Klerk designed the wood panelling and the furniture, as well as the

Front facade of Shipping House, now Hotel Amrâth

Sculpture designs for Shipping House by Michel de Klerk, 1912

Boardroom of the Netherlands Steamship Company, interior by Michel de Klerk and Piet Kramer, circa 1919

The first block at Spaarndammerplantsoen, circa 1924

carpet, the ceiling lamp and the doors. The fine wood carved bird of paradise – like the peacock a symbol of vanity – adorning the office door is possibly a tongue in cheek reference to the director's vanity. A fine example of a 'Gesamtkunstwerk', the Shipping House demonstrates what modern Amsterdam architects and artists were capable of. As a matter of course, they incorporated the applied arts into the totality of a building and infused it with shipping symbolism. The Shipping House is in fact an all-encompassing ode to shipping and to the Dutch colonies. Yet its lavish ornamentation does not in the least detract from the main composition, instead it gave the building a grandeur befitting the powerful and wealthy shipping companies.

Housing Blocks at Spaarndammerplantsoen

Michel de Klerk's big breakthrough came with his housing blocks in Amsterdam-West. At the request of the Public Works department, architect *Jo van der Mey* drew up an urban development plan in 1912 for the as yet unbuilt part of Spaarndammerbuurt, which private architects were allowed to develop. But things did not go smoothly, because the *Gezondheidscommissie* (Health Committee) objected to Van der Mey's plan. A new plan drawn up for the committee by architect *Joseph Th. J. Cuypers* (the son and successor of Pierre Cuypers) was rejected because it did not sufficiently take into account the interests of the various private property owners involved in the plan. In the end, Van der Mey modified his original plan by widening the streets and extending the housing blocks, after which the Mayor and Executive Board proposed it to the municipal council, where it was reviewed on 29 January 1913. Among the various councillors who still objected was *Floor Wibaut*, at the time a member of the Health Committee. He disapproved of the long streets and the 'unattractive and unpractical angled corners' of some of the

Design for the first block at Spaarndammerplantsoen, corner Oostzaanstraat, 1913

Facade of first block at Spaarndammerplantsoen, circa 1920

blocks. He also argued for lower blocks with fewer layers, naming as an example a block of low-rise housing that Eigen Haard had just realised in the Indische Buurt neighbourhood and for which the councillors had received a viewing invitation. Alderman *Delprat* warded off the objections by arguing that the plan had been drawn up by experts such as engineers of the Public Works department and its aesthetic advisor, architect Van der Mey: 'The plan is good, the direction of the streets is good, the depth of the blocks is good and there is light and air'. After lengthy discussions the municipal council eventually approved the plan by 22 votes to 14. Although the plan was to undergo several minor changes in the rest of the neighbourhood, it would largely determine the structure of Spaarndammerplantsoen.

The First 'Purple' Block

Contractor Klaas Hille and his partner G. Kamphuys were given the lease of a municipally owned building site at Spaarndammerplantsoen. Evidently impressed with Hillehuis, they once again asked Michel de Klerk to create a design.

The first building plans dating from November 1913 reveal that De Klerk continued along the line initiated with Hillehuis. Again, the facade was seen as a totality, but the new building fitted into its surroundings to a much greater extent than Hillehuis, with the facade and the public green blending into one another, as it were. De Klerk lavished much attention on the stairwells, which have sensual shapes, small windows and parabolic shaped gables, giving them an almost human appearance. A diversity of materials was used, including various types of bricks and red tiles on the upper section.

The wooden doors were grouped and abundantly decorated, making it a pleasure to enter through them. Even the rear facades received due attention, something that was highly unusual for private builders.

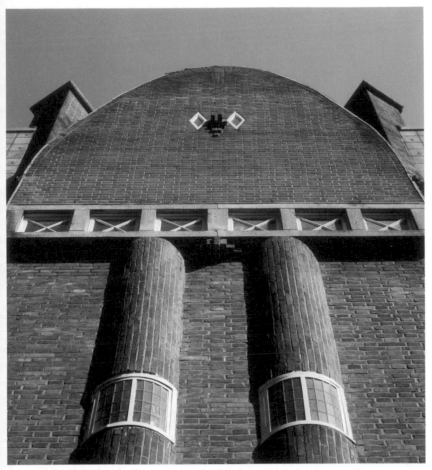

Stairwell of first block at Spaarndammerplantsoen

Decorative element

Striking use of bricks

Sculpture of gnome wearing clogs, with coat of arms of Oostzaan municipality

Doorway of first block

Although De Klerk made some minor adjustments to his sketches, the block was carried out in complete accordance with his ideas. For the corners of the block he designed works of art which he had carried out by sculptor Hildo Krop, a good friend of his. De Klerk drew designs for four different sculptures, including a haystack, a windmill and a country estate, but only the fourth drawing was actually realised. With a touch of De Klerk's humour, it depicts a gnome wearing wooden clogs flanked on either side by a poplar tree. On the Oostzaanstraat side of the block the sculpture bears the coat of arms of the municipality of Oostzaan and on the corner of Krommeniestraat that of Krommenie.

The interior plans of the dwellings were highly unusual, with a large kitchen where the family could eat their meals and a bedroom large enough for daytime use. Both corners of the block had shops with large window-sills where residents could sit down for a chat. Here too, De Klerk had probably been inspired by the small North Holland villages which had given the streets their names and where such 'chat corners' were quite common.

In professional circles, the innovative design of the block attracted a host of conflicting opinions. Newspaper *De Telegraaf* therefore decided it was time for a closer inspection. In a series of articles about architecture published by the newspaper in 1916, the Belgian architect and critic *Huib Hoste* described the housing block as fascinating, both 'in terms of mass and detail'. The building was considered especially intriguing due to its unexpected elements and its colour, creating a sense of anticipation to look further and to 'enjoy'. According to De Telegraaf, this was chiefly due to the fact that De Klerk had in fact treated the block 'as a mass', thereby ensuring that the various components still formed a whole.

The Second 'Yellow' Block

Klaas Hille also asked De Klerk to design the other side of Spaarndammerplantsoen, and once the first block was completed in 1914, he set to work enthusiastically. In the meantime, however, World War One had broken out and although the Netherlands remained neutral it nevertheless felt its effects. Building materials became scarce and expensive, builders were mobilised and tenants could no longer afford the rents being asked for newly built houses. As a result, Klaas Hille could not meet his obligations.

Meanwhile, 1914 also saw Floor Wibaut's appointment as Amsterdam's alderman in charge of housing. Wibaut wished to proceed with building and had ambitious plans to tackle the housing issue and clean up the slums in old parts of the city such as the Jewish quarter, where Michel de Klerk had grown up. The Mayor and Executive Board appointed Wibaut's brother-in-law *Arie Keppler* as the first director of the newly established municipal housing department. Due to the family connection, this decision prompted some criticism from within the council but it was ultimately agreed that Keppler was the best man for the job. Together, Keppler and Wibaut made a powerful duo

The second block at Spaarndammerplantsoen is even more exuberant than the first

Building in Plan Zuid

While The Ship was still in the process of being built, De Klerk was already receiving new assignments. One of these involved *Plan Zuid* (Plan South), Berlage's famous urban development plan for the southern section of the city, which was approved by the city council in 1917. Apart from the bridge across the Amstel river – completed in 1932 – Berlage did not build in Plan Zuid himself but in the spirit of the times Amsterdam School architects were called in.

Michel de Klerk was commissioned to build a new social housing development for housing corporation *De Dageraad* (The Dawn), which, like Like Eigen Haard, had its origins in the labour movement. The corporation had been founded in 1916 by workers' cooperative De Dageraad, which ran a bakery and several shops throughout the city. To help him realise this substantial project, De Klerk called in his friend Piet Kramer. Their tasks were clearly divided, with Kramer being especially responsible for the corners of the blocks at P.L. Takstraat and Burgemeester Tellegenstraat, while De Klerk designed

Dageraad block with imposing organic elements

the two squares as well as the area of P.L. Takstraat situated in between the squares. The sections leading towards the squares and the northern sides of the squares are by Kramer. However, the blocks blend seamlessly, with accentuated features at the beginning of P.L. Takstraat.

Completed between 1922 and 1924, the blocks by De Klerk and Kramer show clear parallels with The Ship. Again, some parts are overhanging, there is an abundant use of bricks and roof tiles, and the buildings are decorated with artistic sculptures, the most striking being the bust of alderman Wibaut, which was unveiled in 1931. A spire designed by De Klerk for the beginning of P.L. Takstraat was never realised, probably due to financial reasons. In its place came curved, stepped corners, each with a stone sculpture by the sculptor *John Rädecker*. With their integrated rounded volumes, these corners are regarded as one of the most spectacular examples of organic architecture.

De Klerk's housing at Thérèse Schwartzeplein and Henriëtte Ronnerplein is equally impressive. Designed to resemble individual country villas, the blocks have a very grand appearance in spite of the fact that the buildings are terraced.

In 1924, engineer *Wattjes* wrote that the De Dageraad housing project had made an 'overwhelming impression' on him. Although he felt there were points of criticism to be made about the other buildings of Plan Zuid, any possible criticism on his part was dispelled upon beholding De Dageraad, leaving only room for the enjoyment and admiration of art: 'Such rich imagination and such restraint in form! Such a grand and monumental objective and how lovingly detailed'.

Like The Ship, the architecture of the new development had a touch of mystery about it. In the *Bouwkundig Weekblad* (Architectural Weekly) of 1923, *J.P. Mieras* asked himself: 'Is it baroque, is it expressionism, is it an act of bravura, is it a profession of faith, is it recklessness or is it proof of mastership?'

Henriëtte Ronnerplein has a villa-like grandeur

Rectangular balconies characterising the facade at Amstellaan, circa 1924

Housing for Private Builders

Within Plan Zuid, Michel de Klerk was also commissioned to design houses at Amstellaan (which is now called Vrijheidslaan) and at Meerhuizenplein. Here, however, the possibilities for extensive detailing and elaborate building constructions were limited. The times had clearly changed. The Dutch government in The Hague was not at all pleased with the high price tag of the buildings that had so far been realised by the various housing corporations and now wished to give private builders more leeway. In Amsterdam South, the association *Amstel's Bouwvereniging* took the initiative to develop part of the district with private builders. *Heere van der Schaar*, the driving force behind this association, had no time for impassioned architects and wished to keep costs down by using standardised house plans. Amsterdam's city council, however, feared a return to the speculative building that preceded the Housing Act and appointed a committee to oversee the quality of *Plan Amstellaan*. This was by no means a superfluous measure, since the contractors made attempts to curb the influence of the architects and for the most part only allowed them to work on the facade, with only the odd contractor commissioning an architect to design an actual floor plan. For most Amsterdam School architects including De Klerk, this conflicted seriously with the principles of their professional ethics. The interior and exterior of a building were of equal importance to these architects; consequently, its architects wished to design a complete building and not just an attractive facade.

In order to keep the wolf from the door, however, the architects accepted the work, Michel de Klerk being no exception. With the limited means at his disposal, he nevertheless managed to deliver an impressive design with wave-like balconies and protruding, rounded bay windows as the most striking elements. At Meerhuizenplein De Klerk reintroduced the rounded elements he had used under the

spire of The Ship at the little square (also known as 'the little bowl')
at Hembrugsstraat. A few years later, architect *J.J.P. Oud* would
incorporate these same shapes into his design of some shops at the
corners of his housing project in Hoek van Holland. It demonstrated
the far-reaching architectural impact of De Klerk's work; even
architects who criticised the Amsterdam School movement and held
completely different architectural principles felt his influence.
Writing about the buildings of Plan Zuid in *Tijdschrift voor
Volkshuisvesting en Stedebouw* (public housing and town planning
magazine) on 15 May 1923, architect *Jan Boterenbrood* applauded
the way in which De Klerk had succeeded in giving Amstellaan an
urban appearance. In contrast with foreign boulevards that all looked
alike, Boterenbrood felt that De Klerk had created a street frontage
along the main road that was just as it should be, 'so purely vivid and
so sensitive' while at the same time being 'very simple'.

Clubhouse De Hoop

The housing blocks of Plan Zuid were to be De Klerk's last major
housing project. Little is known about his personal circumstances
during these years, except that he moved his family to P.C.
Hooftstraat 53 in 1922. This rather posh address has led to
speculation that he was doing well financially, but one should take
into account that the property was located above a horse stable
and that he rented it from his friend Jan Baanders, so the rent was
probably quite reasonable.

That same year De Klerk designed a new clubhouse and boathouse
for the *Koninklijke Amsterdamsche Roei- en Zeilvereeniging 'De
Hoop'* (Royal Amsterdam Boat Club) on the river Amstel. The building
was designed in such a way that it appeared to float above the
waterline. Echoing the shape of the wherry boats used at the club,

At Meerhuizenplein, De Klerk reintroduced the rounded elements he had used for the 'little
bowl' of The Ship, circa 1924

the building was given a long pointed bow, which was however placed perpendicular to the hull. Like The Ship, the clubhouse had various elements that blended together to form a unity. Furthermore, the exterior harmonised perfectly with the interior. Visitors were to feel pleasure upon entering the building and a great deal of attention was therefore paid to the design of the interior and the entrance gate. Critics responded by saying the clubhouse was too beautiful and that sportspeople would consequently be unwilling to take to the water. De Klerk's design also attracted international attention, with the German architect *Erich Mendelsohn* – himself renowned for designing the *Einsteinturm* in Potsdam – describing it as an important masterpiece. Sadly, the clubhouse was demolished at the behest of the German occupiers during World War II, and only the gate and the wherry bow have survived.

During this period, De Klerk also designed his first theatre scenery, having been asked by *Willem Royaards*, director of Nederlands Toneel, to design the sets for their production of Shakespeare's *The Winter Tale*. In addition, he worked on several private residential properties, including a house in Aalsmeer for *A. Barendsen*, a committee member of the Aalsmeer flower auction. De Klerk also designed new premises for the flower auction itself. However, the building required a plain and sober appearance, so it does not display his artistic talents to the full. Further, he worked on the design of a villa in Wassenaar, a new department store for *De Bijenkorf* in The Hague, the restoration of the fire-damaged spire of the Reformed Church in IJsselstein and an emigrant house for Jews who wished to immigrate to Palestine.

Also, when his good friend and colleague architect Guillaume Frédéric La Croix died on 21 July 1923, De Klerk joined up with La Croix's son to design a memorial, which was placed on his grave in Vreeland.

Boathouse for rowing and sailing club De Hoop on the Amstel river

Pointed wherry bow, De Hoop

Brickwork ornamentation on front facade of flower auction hall Aalsmeer

Sudden Death

To De Klerk's disappointment, the villa in Wassenaar never materialised. The emigrant house was not built either, even though the building permit had already been applied for. Piet Kramer would design the new Bijenkorf store and De Klerk's design for the restoration of the church spire in IJsselstein would eventually be carried out by the Baanders practice.

On his 39th birthday – 24 November 1923 – Michel de Klerk died unexpectedly. Photographer *Bernard Eilers*, a good friend who had taken pictures of many of his buildings, took the last picture of him, the saddest of all: 'Michel de Klerk lying in an open coffin in his shroud'. His death came as a tremendous shock. In magazine Wendingen, J.P. Mieras put it as follows: 'It is bitterly harsh that we shall have to miss all the beauty that the future will now keep hidden in its womb'.

A large number of colleagues attended his funeral at Zorgvlied cemetery to pay their last respects. Sadly absent, however, was the architect De Bazel, who died from heart failure during his train journey to the funeral. The sudden loss of two of the country's greatest architects had newspapers and magazines writing of a black day for Dutch architecture. The board members of *Architectura et Amicitia* and the *Bond van Nederlandsche Architecten* (Royal Institute of Dutch Architects) put together a mutual obituary which was enclosed with the December 1923 edition of *Bouwkundig Weekblad* (Architectural Weekly). Herein they expressed their sadness over the loss of 'our greatest architect artist' and 'genius architect'. The 1922 yearbook of *Nederlandsche Ambachts- en Nijverheidskunst* (Dutch Association for Crafts and Industrial Arts), which appeared at the end of 1923, swiftly added an 'In memoriam' by architect Wijdeveld and a wood engraving by artist *Chris Lebeau*. On 29 December 1923, the magazine *Architectura* honoured De Klerk

In Memorian wood engraving by Chris Lebeau

with a special edition dedicated to his memory. Various architects and artists also wrote their own 'In memoriam' to pay their respects to De Klerk. Architect Berlage – often at the receiving end of De Klerk's criticism – described him as the important central figure of 'the Amsterdam direction', which represented a 'liberated architecture' that visitors liked to come and look at. Arie Keppler wrote that Amsterdam had lost its best architect who had done much for social housing and had built landmark buildings of great significance and refinement all over the city. Many pointed to De Klerk's genius and his significance for Amsterdam, with architect *Willem Kromhout* even hailing him as a 'child of the gods'. Just a fortnight before De Klerk's death, the German architect Erich Mendelsohn had visited him and seen some of his work, including his furniture pieces in 't Woonhuys. In newspaper *Berliner Tageblatt* he paid his respects to the Dutch architect, writing that the country 'where the freest architectural ideas prevail' had lost what he considered as its finest young architect, adding that 'We young people from all countries, mourn his loss'. Another such young person was the American architect *Barry Byrne*, who travelled across Europe in the summer of 1924 and wrote home telling of the many talented artists of Amsterdam's interesting, modern, romantic movement. He considered De Klerk to be among the best of these artists, writing that 'his buildings are wonderful' and that his death was 'a very great loss indeed'.

The appreciation for De Klerk did not limit itself to professional circles alone. The social-democratic newspaper *Het Volk* quoted residents of buildings he had designed who thanked De Klerk for what he had done for the working classes. One woman said it was a privilege to live in one of De Klerk's buildings and have her children grow up there. The paper's daily column *Oproerige krabbels* dated 26 November 1923 underlined the importance of Michel de Klerk for workers. The colours and lines of the streets he designed sent out the powerful signal that workers should not be living in bleak and barren neighbourhoods, but that they were entitled to 'vigorous beauty'. Also writing in Het Volk, alderman Wibaut stated that the most beautiful aspect of De Klerk's work was 'the love, purity, passion and utter harmony between the biggest lines and the tiniest details'.

De Klerk's colleague architects took upon themselves the responsibility for his family and saw to it that his widow Lea found work as a secretary at Architectura et Amicitia. In addition, money was raised and a fund set up to purchase De Klerk's drawings so that the family would have financial elbowroom.

Like many other Jews in Amsterdam, Lea did not, however, survive World War II; she died in the concentration camp Auschwitz on 19 November 1942. The couple's son Edo met the same fate and perished in Sobibor on 2 April 1943, leaving only their other son Joost, who died in 2003.

Michel de Klerk's death is widely regarded as a breaking point in the Amsterdam School movement. It brought to an end the opulent expressionistic architecture of blocks such as The Ship and De

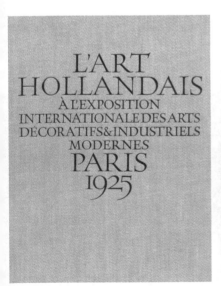

Paris Exhibition, 1925

Dutch Pavilion at Paris exhibition, inspired by the meeting hall of The Ship

Dageraad. The movement was nevertheless well represented at the 1925 *L'Exposition Internationale des Arts Décoratifs et Industriels Modernes* (world exhibition of decorative arts and modern industry in Paris), an event which helped promote the international arts movement *Art Deco*, then very much at its peak. Architect Frits Staal, who had been one of De Klerk's best friends, built the Dutch pavilion, which was clearly inspired by the meeting hall in the courtyard of The Ship. On display in the pavilion were works of art by Dutch artists. Michel de Klerk was posthumously honoured with photographs of his buildings and there was a special salon where his furniture was exhibited.

With the Paris exhibition, the architects of the Amsterdam School attained even greater international prominence. The Paris-based French magazine *L'architecture vivante* devoted most of its 1926 summer edition to 'L'ecole d'Amsterdam'. As well as an editorial about the Amsterdam School movement by chief editor *Jean Badovici*, the magazine published 24 large photographs of Amsterdam School buildings, including two pictures of The Ship, three other buildings by De Klerk and several drawings of the clubhouse for De Hoop. However, the French magazine was not universally laudatory and also expressed some criticism of the Amsterdam School. That is to say, Badovici felt that De Klerk could have had a more profound influence if he had let himself be guided less by the spirit of works from the past.

Furniture, fireplace and wall panelling by Michel de Klerk at the Paris world exhibition, 1925

HIGHLIGHT THE SHIP

The third housing block at Spaarndammerplantsoen was completed in various phases between September 1920 and February 1921. Due to its shape and the multitude of details bringing to mind a ship and the sea, the building soon became known locally as *Het Schip* (The Ship). The front part evokes the bow of a ship and the entire building features recurring wave elements. Also reminiscent of a ship are the outward sloping windows.

Architecture

The Ship was built on a triangular site and has four distinctively individual characters; the low-rise, extravagant, blunt part at Spaarndammerplantsoen, the secluded little square at Hembrugstraat and the two connecting lateral facades. In accordance with De Klerk's ideas, the building's different faces spring from the ever-changing spatial environment of the sides of the triangle.

The point – or apex – of the triangle cuts into the spatial Spaarndammerplantsoen but does more besides. For anybody approaching the building from the Zaanstraat direction, the building looms up in the middle of the road rather like a beacon. On arrival, the road splits to turn around both sides of the building. Architecturally, the extrovert character of this forepart, with its slightly oval turret, striking dark roof tiles as facade cladding and folded, outwardly thrust facade parts and windows, reflects the prominent position of the building. With its great imaginative appeal, this part not only resembles the bow of a ship but is also evocative of a steam locomotive.

The spatial position of the rear of the building is the complete opposite. In an ingenious manner, De Klerk indented the facade, thus creating a small intimate public square. Here, the roof tiles are not strikingly dark but a pleasant orange colour. Used as facade covering, they are drawn down to a very low level and thus form a large expanse of roof, which further contributes to the sense of charm. Rising up above this idyllic little square and completing the picture is the monumental spire, which stands out as the landmark of the neighbourhood and forms its beating heart.

The building's strength lies in its ability to balance and unite its two characters, with the heavy front finding its counterpart in the slender rear. De Klerk has here succeeded in lifting the organic connection between the parts to the highest possible level; two opposing but complementary characters are united in one total work.

In marking the transition between the building's two beacons, the lateral five storey facades in orange brick form the block's binding elements and are therefore essential for the character of the building as a whole. De Klerk subtly imbued these masses with highly dynamic almost wave-like properties, doing so differently in Zaanstraat than in Oostzaanstraat.

The lateral facades from which the extrovert front arises have a robustly horizontal composition. In the Oostzaanstraat facade this is slightly less obvious due to the already existing school around which The Ship was built. At the Zaanstraat side the orange brick facade stretches across the entire length and is overtly horizontal in composition. It is striking to see how the three bands of vertically placed bricks actually empasise the facade's horizontal character. These bands are accentuated further by the small five-sided stairwell windows positioned within them. With their angles pointing outwards, these windows add an extra sense of rhythm.

At the little square at Hembrugstraat, the horizontal aspect of the brick facade is combined with vertically protruding round corners on each side. These impart the square with a sense of balance and almost seem to guide passers-by to the front doors.

Building work on The Ship with the already completed Zaanhof in the background, 1919

Building plan for The Ship

Building work on The Ship, circa 1919

Detailing of Design and Ornamentation

The Ship forms a unity even though its facade has different characteristics and details; it has a clear composition while simultaneously showing great diversity. This is the DNA of The Ship, ensuring that the building never becomes tedious. The detailing of the facade and the use of ornamentation shed a great deal of light upon De Klerk's artistry. What we see here is not an urge for ornamentation gone out of control but rather a case of the details contributing to the composition as a whole.

De Klerk was very particular about the design of his windows, paying special attention not only to the shapes but also to the use of materials and the arrangement of the glazing bars. Apart from some metal window frames, most of the window frames in The Ship are made of wood. Most of the panes are made of glass while leaded glass was used for some of the stairwell windows and wired glass for the small windows in the doors. Although so-called ladder windows are the predominant type, the building also has windows with a completely different arrangement. The outwardly protruding windows at the folds of the 'bow', for example, have vertical bars while some of the small stairwell windows consist of diagonally placed bars. With their parabolic shape and their own unique glazing bar pattern, the large post office windows at Zaanstraat and Oostzaanstraat are especially unique.

In order to reinforce their various characters, several windows and doors have finely detailed ornamentation, such as the attractive ribbed finish on one side of some of the windows. Also, the recurrence of several striking elements additionally underlines the building's sense of unity. Examples include the unique hoisting shutters in the attics, the dark, vertically placed bricks marking the building's base and the dark roof tiles which stretch across the facade in horizontal lines and also adorn the upper part of the turret

The district post office in The Ship was visible from afar, circa 1925

at the post office entrance. Further, there are numerous recurring geometric shapes, such as the parabolic shape of the post office windows that reappears in the archway entrance to the inner court behind the post office and continues in a smaller version in the first doorway porch. Similarly, the five-sided stairwell windows along the long Zaanstraat frontage are repeated in the extension above the school. What's more, the base of the spire is pentagon shaped. There are several places where the ornamentation does not directly contribute to the composition but where the building and its spatial environment simply begged to be enhanced with a decorative touch. A wonderful example are the birds sculpted in brick at the post office corner. Settled on the most peaceful spot they oversee the entire Spaarndammerplantsoen. The two Zaan windmills designed in natural stone at Oostzaanstraat are equally pleasing, and form a beautiful tribute to the street's name.

The Post Office
The Ship consisted of 102 dwellings with a district post office on the ground floor at Spaarndammerplantsoen. This post office could be seen from afar due to the round turret above its entrance, its black tiled upper reminiscent of the chimney pipes on the many large steam ships of the time. People were supposed to enjoy going there, so De Klerk designed the inside of the post office with great attention to detail. As well as a maple wood floor and a trapezium-shaped ceiling, the interior has a carefully chosen colour scheme, with the lavender blue tiles in the visitor's section giving it a distinctive and monumental character. Jugendstil influences can be found both in the upper sections of the counters – which are partly made of wrought iron – and in the door hinges. De Klerk even designed the letters of the descriptive signs in the post office.

Important elements in the post office were the telephone booth and the speaking booth. In those days, workers could not afford a telephone at home so besides going to the post office to buy stamps or deposit money into their *Rijkspostspaarbank* account, they went there to make telephone calls. This was a rather laborious affair. First the caller had to give the required number to the postal worker, who dialled the number in the telephone booth behind. Then the caller would wait on the bench until a connection had been established. Once this was the case the telephone could be heard ringing and the caller could enter the speaking booth and have the conversation. To guarantee privacy, De Klerk created double doors for sound insulation, even providing them with a felt finishing. Both the booth and door have leaded glass windows, with bars clearly representing telegraph wires and little birds perched on top. In all likelihood, the birds are a humorous reference to the Dutch word 'luistervink', which translates as eavesdropper but literally means 'listen finch'. De Klerk's humourous touch can also be found in other details such as the truncheon which has been integrated into the sign that reads 'verboden' (prohibited), indicating that visitors were not to enter the postal sorting area. With the passing of time this truncheon disappeared, but it has recently been reconstructed and is back in its original place.

De Klerk used a more elevated form of art to decorate the entrance of the post office. Above the door the house number 38 was carved from stone with a sort of trunk or snake underneath. It somewhat resembles the mythical 'makara', a hybrid creature with the body of a fish and the head of an elephant that can sometimes be seen on Indian temples.

Notwithstanding the unique interior of the new post office, the postal service *PTT* (Post Telegraaf en Telefoon) showed little inclination to actually move in after its completion in 1920. The rent

Stamp 'De leeuw in de Hollandse tuin', designed by Michel de Klerk

PTT coat of arms, designed by Michel de Klerk

charged by Eigen Haard was considered far too high and the post office remained empty for some time. Due to its specific design and purpose, however, it could not be put to other use, so Eigen Haard eventually lowered the rent and PTT took up residence there after all. Contrary to what one might expect, this did not negatively affect De Klerk's collaboration with PTT. The postal services held graphic design in high regard and also gave him other assignments, including two coats of arms for PTT, the largest of which hung outside many post offices for years. De Klerk also designed an unusual letter box with a monkey sitting on top of it, its lips sealed with a lock. This served to indicate that PTT took good care of people's letters and that residents could safely entrust their letters to the box. The letter box, the prototype of which still exists, never went into production because it was a cast iron, built-in letter box and PTT anticipated problems if public letter boxes were placed into post office walls. When PTT invited Michel de Klerk to take part in a competition to design stamps he submitted two entries. His design for a five guilder stamp, depicting Queen Wilhelmina with a laughing, crowned lion on her back was, however, considered too frivolous. Although impressed with the quality of the design, the jury felt it could not be issued, their reason being that the queen's neck was too thin. De Klerk was asked to draw a more worthy queen which he later did, but the new design was not used either. His other entry, a design for a two cent stamp, won him second prize and was titled *De leeuw in de Hollandse tuin* (The lion in the Dutch garden). Michel's son Joost later said that in the De Klerk household, the stamp was always referred to as 'the lion in the cherry basket'. There are two versions of the issued stamp, a violet blue 1 cent stamp and an orange-red 2 cent stamp. Just like his buildings, De Klerk's stamp designs were highly detailed. It is only on second glance that one sees that the stamp depicts a Dutch lion, sitting on a wicker cherry basket in a garden full of flowers and fruit.

View from post office desk towards the waiting bench and speaking booth

Post office gable stone bearing a post-horn

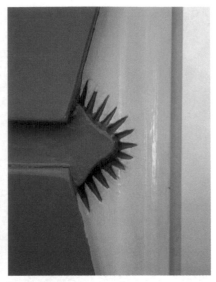

Detail of telephone booth

Telephone booth in the post office

The Ship's 'hold', with a view of the meeting hall and the spire in the background, circa 1924

The Inner Court

Outside the post office De Klerk designed rectangular gable stones
– also rather like stamps - with symbolic references to the postal
services, including a post-horn and a lightning bolt. As was the
case with De Klerk's first block, these artistic elements were in
all probability designed by De Klerk and later executed by the city
sculptor Hildo Krop.

Behind the post office De Klerk created a long, parabolic shaped
archway offering access to a secluded inner court. Above the post
office windows is a sculpture depicting two small animals. Some
people claim they are greyhounds symbolising the speed of the postal
services but they could also be interpreted as marsupials, their
pouches representing the filled satchels of the postmen.

The inner court of The Ship fits into the tradition of courts found in
medieval Europe – such as the Begijnhof in the city centre – except
that it is much smaller and has a more modern spatial design. Inside,
De Klerk located just ten dwellings, each with their own specific
design. Some of the bay windows overhang the private gardens

below and after dark the lamps of opaline glass placed on the two pillars provide enchanting light. The little square itself is paved in a compass pattern using yellow IJssel clinkers.

What makes the little court so special is that residents passing through the archway suddenly enter an entirely different world, where the hustle and bustle of everyday life disappears. Architect Willem Kromhout, known for his art nouveau style *Hotel Americain* at Leidseplein, was deeply impressed with this tranquility when he once passed through the archway: 'All things passionate and poetic that the past has left us by way of courts, squares, streets and alleys are united here, greatly, profoundly and harmoniously, with a rare command of material, line and colour'.

Architect *Aug. M.J. Sevenhuijsen* also seems to have been full of admiration for De Klerk's court. In 1927 he wrote the introduction to the book *Nieuwe bouwkunst in Nederland* (new Dutch architecture), which not only contained several photographs of The Ship but also had the little court prominently featured on its title page.

Meeting Hall

In the inner courtyard, De Klerk designed small sheds for the private gardens as well as a larger meeting hall, which was accessible only by a narrow path. Built at the same time as the rest of The Ship, the meeting hall fits perfectly with the main building and is even organically connected to it by means of a small wall that runs along the gardens of the residents. Sometimes referred to as 'the captain's dwelling', the meeting hall forms the heart of The Ship.

The meeting hall functioned as a place where the board of the housing corporation could hold their consultation hours and where residents could organise activities. At the time, Eigen Haard was a real association, which meant that in addition to rent the tenants

The archway entrance to the courtyard

The inner courtyard of The Ship, circa 1924

also paid membership fees, practically making them co-owners with duties as well as rights. They were expected to behave properly and observe the rules and regulations – over 20 – listed in the tenancy agreement. Keeping pigeons or beating carpets in the inner courtyard was not allowed, for example. Also, residents were frequently addressed by the board about wet laundry hanging out to dry on the verandas, as this could annoy downstairs neighbours. One of the important ideals of the association was that residents were to help one another and for this reason each housing complex owned by Eigen Haard had a residents' committee, the members of which were elected by the residents of the block in question. In the meeting hall, The Ship's resident's committee organised wood sawing for children, dancing for the young folk and card games for adults. One of the highlights was the 'red berry feast' held by Eigen Haard each year towards the end of the summer. During this event, the resident's committee would take children from The Ship to the Watergraafsmeer neighbourhood, where they joined children from other housing blocks for a big feast and were treated to vitamin-packed red berries.

Every now and then, the resident's committee would collectively purchase potatoes and fuel in order to save money. These were stored in the meeting hall and later distributed among the residents. There was also a small library where residents could borrow books.

Sketch of little meeting hall for Eigen Haard Housing Corporation

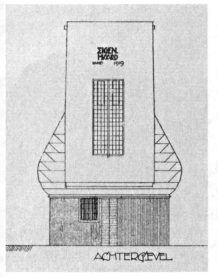

Rear facade of meeting hall

Brickwork typography on rear facade of meeting hall

De Klerk designed the meeting hall in such a way that made these various uses possible in spite of the limited space. During consultation hours, residents could wait on a bench in a small waiting area. The meeting room itself had a modest size but the high wooden ceiling and large beams created a sense of space. In order to highlight the building's purpose it had the name Eigen Haard on it in large brick letters with the year of contruction '1920' underneath.

The Spire

With The Ship, Michel de Klerk created a unique building that made a bold statement: namely, that workers were entitled to good quality, beautiful dwellings. It thereby displays the strength of the workers' movement from which Eigen Haard emerged. In one of his draft sketches, De Klerk designed the two brick chimneys on top of the building as two clenched fists – a symbol of the workers' struggle – but eventually he changed them into lion heads with teeth and manes. Nevertheless, the chimneys still bear a faint resemblance to two fists. The symbolism of the spire is of a more abstract kind; it shows that the workers' movement had the courage to make itself known. Also, it is probably no coincidence that a Catholic church with a large spire (the *Maria Magdalenakerk* by Pierre Cuypers) was located on a similar triangular plot of land nearby. The Eigen Haard workers now had their very own – albeit smaller – spire and its fine shape helped them to step out proudly and show society that a new dawn had risen. Compared to the spires of Amsterdam, that of The Ship had a highly new and stylised shape. De Klerk had clearly been inspired by spires elsewhere in the world, particularly that of the *Paladshotel* in Copenhagen, which he had sketched during one of his trips.

The Ship at Hembrugstraat, circa 1923

De Klerk's spire had a highly ingenious contruction with its framework consisting entirely of wooden rafters and its exterior clad with red roof tiles. Initially, De Klerk wished to have a rooster and clock adorning his spire. Why these were not realised remains unknown; it may have been due to a shortage of funds or perhaps he just changed his mind. In the end the spire was topped with a wrought iron tree of life. This ancient symbol, common to many places including the nearby Zaan region, indicates that something is growing and blooming within the building.

The spire of The Ship captured everybody's imagination and its picture would later make its way into many magazines and books. The Christmas 1926 issue of magazine *Op De Hoogte* published pen drawings of The Ship with the spire resembling a twinkling diamond. In the accompanying text, *A. van der Boom* wrote of the pure manner in which De Klerk had managed to have the spaces grow and described the 'virginally delicate spire' as the symbol of De Klerk's talent, adding that it could rightly be called 'De Klerk's spire'.

In the first edition of a twenty-part series of monographs on modern Dutch architecture published from 1932 onwards, architect Jan Gratama described the spire as masterly. He said the spire came forth purely from 'emotional motives' because having no purpose or function, 'it underlines, in its stagnancy and thinness, the flowing and monumental character of the high-rise building, while vice versa the robustness of the high-rise sections, especially expressive in the lateral facades, reinforces the decorative and upward shooting character of the spire'.

One of De Klerk's designs for the spire

Framework of wooden rafters within the spire

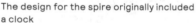

The design for the spire originally included a clock

The spire above the 'little bowl'

The Rembrandt of Architecture

A Belgian architect who visited The Ship in 1920 considered it a very peculiar building indeed. In newspaper *Le Soir* he wrote that viewing it made him feel like he was going delirious. Furthermore, the building reminded him somewhat of the strange stories by the Belgian writer and Nobel Prize winner *Maurice Maeterlinck*, particularly his play *La Princesse Maleine*.

In the city council, the high cost and opulent appearance of The Ship raised questions, with some councillors saying that The Ship was too luxurious for workers to live in. During a council meeting on 8 October 1920, alderman Wibaut found himself in a position where he had to stoutly defend the cost of the building. A great lover of art, Wibaut was chairman of the association *Kunst aan het Volk* while his wife *Mathilde Berdenis van Berlekom* was a well-known author of children's books. Their children shared their parents' love for the arts and daughter Josina was married to the son of Vincent van Gogh's brother. The Wibaut family recognised De Klerk's talent; they had various of his travel sketches on their walls and for many years there was a picture of him on Mathilde's writing desk. Also, one of Wibaut's children was good friends with the De Klerks.

In the city council Wibaut pointed out that Michel de Klerk was an important architect-artist and if they wanted something other than the ordinary they should give him the opportunity to build. He subtly reminded them how he had formed a minority when, as a councillor in 1913, he had voted against the development of Spaarndammerbuurt due to the awkward shape of the angular sites. Now he wished to concede that De Klerk had solved the issue of the 'wondrous shape' of the building site very well indeed. In order to further promote the talents of 'the artist De Klerk', he recounted a story about a lunch he had attended in *Stadsherberg* with a group of Swedes and Norwegians who had come to Amsterdam to view several buildings. During the lunch a chair that had been reserved for a prominent Scandinavian architect remained empty. When Wibaut enquired what was keeping this man he was told that the architect probably wouldn't be coming, since he had remained behind in the dwellings at Spaarndammerplantsoen and could not tear himself away. When Wibaut later spoke to him, the elated Scandinavian architect declared that 'De Klerk is the Rembrandt of architecture'.

Wibaut's plea to the city council made quite an impression. Furthermore, he was supported in the debate by councillor and architect Z. Gulden, who stated that 'generations to come will thank us for this means of urban expansion'. After the Mayor and Executive Board acknowledged that the construction had been 'rather more expensive' than intended but that this would in future be the exception rather than the rule, the city council acquiesced. Thus the criticism over the high costs did not jeopardise the construction of The Ship. Eventually, the proposal that the previously established advance to Eigen Haard of 640,000 guilders be increased by 290,000 guilders was approved without a roll-call vote.

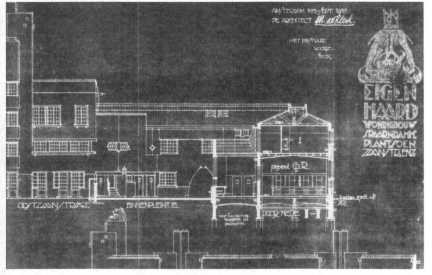

Blueprint cross-section courtyard, 1918

Watercolour impressions of The Ship

Nursery School De Veulens

When Michel de Klerk was commissioned to design The Ship he was faced with a nursery school that had been built on the site in 1915. It had been constructed in a traditional architectural style using the cross bond brickwork pattern highly common at the time, i.e. alternating courses of headers and stretchers with the second course of stretchers offset from the first. Demolition was too expensive so De Klerk created a design with small extensions on both sides above the building. Another plan for which he made a concept sketch involved expanding the school by building an extra storey on top of it, but this proposal met with scepticism from the council; there was no need for extra classrooms and the council was not prepared to spend extra money for expansion on purely aesthetic grounds. Notwithstanding, De Klerk still wanted to integrate the school into The Ship and to that end he designed three-meter high curved volumes above the school. Wood clad window boxes intended for red geraniums were to be placed between these extensions on the school's top floor. Several councillors opposed this idea

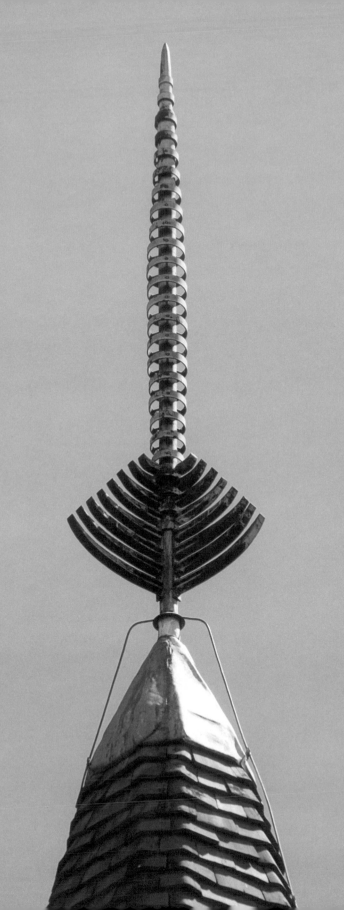

28

113　　but Wibaut replied that he dared predict that one day, 'these red geraniums are looked upon with pleasure, compared to the yellow dandelions of monotonous buildings'.

In 1925 – two years after De Klerk's death – the school was given an extension based on his sketches but also featuring some new architectural additions. The left hand extension was removed, or rather reshaped into an arm-like structure that seems to be tenderly embracing the original school, as it were. Also, some visually disturbing elements present in the original facade were removed. Since the new storey was built using the same orange brick used for The Ship, the housing block became an organic entity. Due in part to the small void between the extensions, the upper volumes appear to be pulling towards one another.

While the old school was in itself a simple dark brick building, the extra storey, the window alterations and the addition of sculptures transformed the facade into a true work of art. Sculptor Hildo Krop was responsible for the foal heads which were added to both the front and the rear facade as a reference to the name which the school carried for many years: *De Veulens* (the foals). Looking like they are about to jump out from the actual walls, Krop's foals represent the youthful frivolity of the school's infants.

Nursery school before it was heightened, circa 1922

The school, circa 2012

Sculpture by Hildo Krop on the school's staircase banister

The nursery school in its original state, circa 1922

Children on the playground, circa 1930

The school was given a new entrance leading to a central hall with an Amsterdam School style stairway, decorated with a wood carving by Hildo Krop. The work of art depicts a foal being tamed by a man, a possible reference to the daily task of the teachers. Above the outside entrance is a granite sculpture of a concentrated archer trying to gather food amid doe deer and flowers, while hidden in a little corner is a small sculpture of a man and a staff, symbolising the shepherd with the staff of wisdom.

The Residents

In The Ship Michel de Klerk gave free reign to his artistic imagination, with no detail escaping his attention. The small windmills referred to the Zaan area which gave the streets their names and the architecture of which had inspired him for The Ship. House numbers with their own unique typography were chiselled out of stone and the year 1919 (when construction started) is indicated in elegant numbers. Windows and doors were carefully designed, as were the floor plans of the dwellings. Some dwellings had their own private entrance while others were grouped in a shared stairway. They were fitted with a mantelpiece, a kitchen, a bedstead and round, built-in cabinets. In all, the block was laid out with 18 different floor plans. Some of these had peculiar shapes much like a half diamond. Most dwellings consisted of two bedrooms, a living room and a kitchen. The kitchens were quite large by early twentieth century standards, the thinking behind this being that small families could eat their meals there and thus keep the living room clean and tidy.

The residents took great pride in their complex, a fact illustrated by an appeal made by the residents' committee in 1925 in Eigen Haard's monthly magazine, calling on children to refrain from drawing on the walls with chalk, since the blocks 'due to their remarkable construction, attract the attention of passers-by'. The committee also took action itself: 'On our part we will soon set to remove election posters and other irregularities to make our houses presentable from the outside'. Following De Klerk's death, one female resident described the buildings at Spaarndammerplantsoen as a dream and a fairy tale for children: 'Is it not wonderful to return from the weariness of the day to a house of pure pleasure and domestic bliss? Is it not as if every brick calls out to you: Come all you workers and rest in your homes, which have been made for you. Is the Spaarndammerplantsoen not the fairy tale you dreamt of as a child, since it was something we children never had?'

In the members' magazine, an Eigen Haard committee member commented on The Ship's construction method and its use of various materials by acknowledging that although the building was attractive,

Eigen Haard stock certificate, 1935

Kitchen in The Ship with granite worktop, circa 1965

Newly married young couple at the archway

the corporation would probably be paying for it for many years to come. He feared its maintenance constituted a potentially 'heavy burden' for the corporation. In hindsight, such fears were not entirely unfounded, since Eigen Haard has to invest a great deal of money in the building's maintenance to this day.

When The Ship was completed, its new residents were mostly made up of relatively well-off workers employed in municipal departments such as the gas company, the tramway or the water works. The rents being charged in the new housing block varied from three to five guilders a week, which was quite expensive in those days. Eigen Haard ensured that the sums owing were paid on time by sending a rent collector round on a fixed day each week to collect the money. Carrying a black bag, he would stand in the street and loudly call out the names of the tenants.

Casual labourers working at the docks and labourers without a fixed employment contract could not afford to live in The Ship. For this less well-off group, the municipal housing service built more basic dwellings at Zaandammerplein, with sculleries instead of kitchens. This part of the Spaarndammerbuurt neighbourhood

Children playing around The Ship, circa 1939

became predominantly communist while residents of The Ship generally supported the social democratic workers party *SDAP*. The children living in The Ship often joined the social-democratic youth organisation *AJC* (Arbeiders Jeugd Centrale) which organised all kinds of activities ranging from film evenings and pleasant nature walks to an annual camping outing to Paasheuvel on the Veluwe.

Contemporary Publications

Once The Ship was completed the result captured everybody's imagination. Architects from other parts of the Netherlands such as Groningen, Friesland and Brabant became increasingly inspired by Michel de Klerk and also started to build in the style of the Amsterdam School. Apart from residential buildings, they built churches, schools and even farmhouses incorporating elements influenced by The Ship.

At this point, the Amsterdam School was featured in just about every book on Dutch public housing or architecture, and this helped make Amsterdam the 'mecca of public housing'. In the magazine

119   *Architectural Review* of August 1922, an article by *Howard Robertson* titled 'Modern Dutch Architecture' paid considerable attention to the newly completed Ship. Accompanying the piece were seven large photographs of the blocks at Spaarndammerplantsoen, taken by F.R. Yerbury. According to the author, Michel de Klerk was a 'shining star' who exercised an enormous influence on modern Dutch architects. Robertson heaped praise on the housing blocks at Spaarndammerplantsoen, being especially impressed with De Klerk's striking use of bricks: 'Broad swept curves, tiny apsidal turrets, chevron arrises and string-courses, bricks in chequer, wave, herringbone, and vertical pattern, all are conceived and executed with a perfection which places the modern Dutch builder in the forefront of technicians and craftsmen.' As well as applauding De Klerk's imagination and skill, Robertson expressed his deep respect for the director of the municipal housing service (Arie Keppler), for making it all possible.

De Klerk's buildings were also featured in the November 1924 issue of the Italian magazine *Architettura e Arti Decorative*, which published seven photographs including one of the spire at Hembrugstraat and a romantic photo of the inner court. The author of the piece, architect Gaetano Minnucci, made it clear to his readers that there was more to the Netherlands besides windmills and canals, adding that Italy could learn from the unique, modern style of architecture that had evolved in the Netherlands.

The courtyard, circa 1925

120   Although critical remarks concerning the cost of The Ship had not
       yet abated within Amsterdam's city council, there was nevertheless a
       great sense of pride over the new buildings that had been realised in
       the city.
       In November 1924, Amsterdam hosted the *International Congress
       for Housing and City Planning*, which included various discussions
       about public housing presided by Wibaut, now alderman for Finance.
       Architects and public housing officials from all over the world were
       taken on bus tours to view the city's new neighbourhoods and were
       much astonished when they saw The Ship.

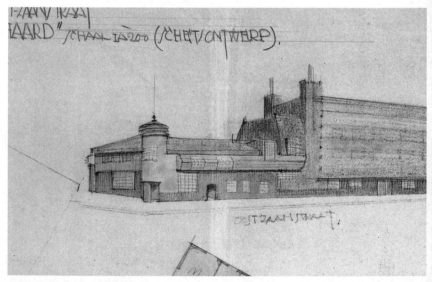

Design drawing of The Ship

RE-EVALUATION

The Amsterdam School and The Ship in particular remain a source of inspiration right up to the present day. In recent years, the architect's personal expression and creative power, as epitomised by Michel de Klerk and other Amsterdam School architects, is once again being brought to the fore. A new expressionist movement can clearly be discerned in contemporary architecture, with sculptural shapes, theatrical curves and ornaments making their comeback. In its expressive play of shapes however, The Ship remains unequalled.

The Response from the Nieuwe Bouwen Movement

It is certainly difficult to imagine today that there was a period of many years when the Amsterdam School – and The Ship with it – went largely unappreciated. With the passing of time, criticism of the Amsterdam School began to grow. The artist *Theo van Doesburg* wrote a letter bemoaning the fact that a modern Dutch art movement like *De Stijl* was inadequately represented at the Paris world exhibition. In 1925 two incensed articles appeared in the German architecture magazine *Wasmuths Monatshefte für Baukunst*. Titled 'From the Amsterdam Chamber of Horrors', one of the articles denounced the 'extravagances and unbusinesslike expressionism' of the Amsterdam School. According to its author *Werner Hegemann*, the most objectionable part was that 'such whims' and 'architectural opulence' were not being implemented 'for a crazy millionaire but for public housing'. Michel de Klerk, who, much to Hegemann's indignation, had been lauded in the *Stuttgarter Bauzeitung* of 25 March 1925, was a particular object of his venom. He described him not as an architect but as a 'gifted, undisciplined and insane draughtsman'.

Ideas about architecture were clearly changing and the new *Bauhaus* movement, which originated in Weimar, was becoming more influential. In the Netherlands the new notions evolved into the functionalist *Nieuwe Bouwen* (New Building) movement, with *Cornelis van Eesteren*, *Ben Merkelbach* and *Mart Stam* as its leading figures. As the young Amsterdam School architects had criticised Berlage, so the New Building figures found fault with the Amsterdam School, distancing themselves from it in their manifestos and in their magazine *De 8 en Opbouw*. Proclaiming its opposition to 'opulent architecture springing from the obsession with form of talented individuals', the new movement denounced the Amsterdam School architects for lacking all self-control and branded them as 'draughtsmen' indulging in excessive individual artistic expression. The architects associated with De 8 en Opbouw wanted to return to the basics of architecture and pleaded for a rationalist and functionalist style of architecture that made use of modern technological developments.

Weissenhofsiedlung, a housing development built in Stuttgart in 1927 in an utterly new style with lots of light, air, space and glass, was a major source of inspiration. Architects involved included *Le Corbusier*, *Mies van der Rohe* and *Walter Gropius*, as well as Dutch architects such as Mart Stam and Jacob Johannes Oud.

Some of the New Building principles were put into practice in 1936 in the Amsterdam neighbourhood *Landlust*, where architects Ben

Square in front of the post office, circa 1995

Magazine of the Nieuwe Bouwen movement, 1937

Merkelbach, *Charles Karsten* and *Piet Vorkink* introduced detached perimeter housing blocks looking out on to a green area. The project was a breakthrough for New Building and signalled a definite end to the Amsterdam School period.

By the late 1920's, people's appreciation for the buildings created by the Amsterdam School architects was diminishing dramatically. The 1929 standard work *Modern Architecture, romanticism and reintegration* by *Henry Russell Hitchcock* was probably one of the last books of the period to be reasonably positive about the Amsterdam School. Hitchcock expressed great admiration for the 'amazing skill' with which De Klerk used bricks and roof tiles to create various patterns and remarked that it gave surfaces a textile-like quality. Also, he felt that De Klerk's buildings were lively and expressive, partly due to the unique arrangement of windows and use of ornamentation.

S. Giedeon, the secretary of the international architectural organization *CIAM (Congrès Internationaux d'Architecture Modernes)* which had been founded in 1928, was less appreciative

Renovation work on The Ship, 1977–1980

of the Amsterdam School movement. In his famous 1941 book *Space, time and architecture*, he dismissed architectural expressionism as 'general insecurity' and the only mention of Michel de Klerk in the book referred to the more functionalist housing block he had built at Amstellaan.

Renewed Interest

It was not until long after World War II, in the 1970's, that a renewed interest for the Amsterdam School emerged in the Netherlands. Nieuwe Bouwen had meanwhile lost its lustre and a new quest for the human touch became perceptible under the influence of architects and artists such as *Constant Nieuwenhuys* and *Aldo van Eyck*. Residents protested against the large-scale demolition of old neighbourhoods and managed to prevent an important share of Amsterdam School buildings from being pulled down. There was a revived appreciation for the sincere warmth of The Ship and Eigen Haard called in architects practice *H. van Straalen* to carry out extensive renovations on the building, which commenced in 1977. Renovation work came not a moment too soon as The Ship had fallen into serious disrepair, with the spire at the little square in danger of collapse. In addition, the needs of residents had changed considerably over the years, with people wanting more space, central heating and room for a washing machine or tumble dryer. To this end, several dwellings were merged into larger apartments, leaving 82 of the original 102 dwellings. The interiors of the dwellings changed dramatically, with the old granite worktops in the kitchens being replaced by Bruynzeel kitchens and the floors raised so that it was easier for residents to look out of the windows. When the renovation plans were drawn up there was a great deal of discussion about the small windows, with some residents complaining that they found it difficult to clean them and suggesting they be replaced by modern panes. Fortunately, the Amsterdam School had meanwhile rehabilitated sufficiently for this proposal to be rejected. State secretary *Jan Schaefer* – who would later become an Amsterdam alderman – personally devoted himself to collecting money for the renovation, appealing not only to public housing grants but also to arts and culture subsidies. Describing The Ship as a 'monument of the workers' , Schaefer felt that the high cost of renovation was justified in every respect.
The renovation work on The Ship took about 400 working days. On 15 February 1980, minister *Beelaerts van Blokland* paid a personal visit to The Ship to hand over the keys of the last apartment to be renovated. The Ship had been restored to its former glory and was a building to be proud of once more. It was listed as a Rijksmonument (national heritage building) and even recreated in model form to be given a prominent spot in the miniature city Madurodam.

Stream of Publications

Remarkably enough, the renewed appreciation of the Amsterdam School was set in motion outside the Netherlands. In 1968, the Italian *Giovanni Fanelli* wrote a comprehensive book about *Moderne architectuur in Nederland* (modern architecture in the Netherlands), the first publication in years to pay considerable attention to the Amsterdam School. Michel de Klerk was back in the limelight too, after *Suzanne Frank* wrote an extensive monograph on his life and work for the University of Columbia, New York in 1969.

In the Netherlands, the revival of the Amsterdam School was ushered in by *J.J. Vriend*, who, after previous publications, wrote a monograph on the subject in 1970. Three years later, *Ons Amsterdam* magazine had a special theme issue about the Amsterdam School, followed in 1975 by a major exhibition at Amsterdam's *Stedelijk Museum*. The exhibition attracted a great deal of interest and was accompanied by an extensive catalogue and a walking and cycling route through the city. The fascination with the Amsterdam School also continued to grow abroad, with the prestigious Japanese magazine *Global Architecture (GA)* devoting its entire 56th edition to the social housing blocks built by Michel de Klerk for Eigen Haard and De Dageraad. In New York, Dutchman *Wim de Wit* put together

Cover of Global Architecture, no. 56

Maristella Casciato
Wim de Wit

**Le case
Eigen Haard
di De Klerk**

1913/21

Tihanyi Judit – Halmos György

AZ **AMSZTERDAMI
ISKOLA** 1910–1930

J. J. Vriend   Arte plástico y arquitectura en holanda

La Escuela de Amsterdam

**Michel de Klerk
1884-1923**
An Architect of the
Amsterdam School

Suzanne S. Frank

**UMI Research Press
Studies in the Fine Arts:Architecture**

Nederlandse architectuur

1910-1930

AMSTERDAMSE
SCHOOL

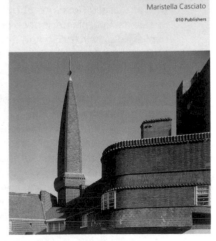

The Amsterdam School
Maristella Casciato
010 Publishers

Publications about the Amsterdam School, Michel de Klerk and The Ship

The post office with letterbox and phone booth, 1979

an exhibition focussing on the Amsterdam School for the *Cooper-Hewitt Museum* in New York; this was the first major exhibition on the movement to be organised outside the Netherlands. Following on from this exhibition, De Wit collaborated with others to publish the 1983 book *The Amsterdam School*, subtitled *Dutch expressionist architecture 1915-1930*. In 1984 he also co-authored a book with *Maristella Casciato* about Eigen Haard's housing blocks at Spaarndammerplantsoen: *Le case Eigen Haard di De Klerk*, which was published only in Italian and never translated. Casciato's 1987 book *La Scuola di Amsterdam*, however, was translated both into Dutch and English and was for many years considered a standard work on Amsterdam School architecture. Many more publications would follow in various languages; there is even a book about Amsterdam School architecture in Hungarian.

A stream of publications have also appeared in the Netherlands and the movement's trailblazer Michel de Klerk is once again the subject of much interest. In the summer of 1997, the *Netherlands Architecture Institute (NAI)* in Rotterdam, which has an extensive archive of his drawings and travel sketches, organised a large retrospective exhibition of De Klerk's work. In conjunction with the exhibition *Manfred Bock*, *Vladimir Stissi* and *Sigrid Johannisse* wrote a book with in-depth considerations of Michel de Klerk's buildings.

Museum

In 2001, the centennial anniversary of the Housing Act of 1901 was celebrated in the Netherlands. In allowing the construction of good quality and beautiful housing for workers, this act formed an important basis for the Amsterdam School to come to fruition. As part of the celebrations, the post office in The Ship – which was in use until 1999 – had its interior entirely restored and reopened as a museum dedicated to the Amsterdam School: *Museum Het Schip*. This aroused such interest that it was also decided to reconstruct a worker's dwelling as originally designed by De Klerk, straight under the famous spire. The museum now offers daily guided tours around De Klerk's three building blocks at Spaarndammerplantsoen. In addition, visitors can view exhibitions about the Amsterdam School and see street furniture in the museum garden. Museum Het Schip is growing and seeing a steady increase in the number of visitors, not only from the Netherlands, but from all over the world.

Entrance to the museum in The Ship, 2012

Tourist sign at Museum Het Schip

Interior of museum residence

The waiting bench beside the speaking booth, also designed by Michel de Klerk

The speaking booth in the museum

BIBLIOGRAPHY

Architectura et Amicita and Bond van Nederlandsche Architecten: *Necrologie* (enclosed with Bouwkundig Weekblad, December 1923)

Architectenbureau H. van Straalen B.N.A.: *Renovatie 't Schip Amsterdam* (Zeist 1980)

Badovici, Jean: *L'Ecole d'Amsterdam* (L'Architecture Vivante, summer 1926, year 4, no. 12, p. 21-27)

Baroni, Daniele e Antonio D'Auria: *Michel de Klerk, protagonisti del Movimento moderno* (Ottagono, 64, marzo 1982, 26-33)

Bergvelt, Ellinoor et al.: *De Amsterdamse School 1910-1930* (Amsterdam 1975)

Berlage, H.P.: *M. de Klerk* (Architectura, 29 December 1923, p.230)

Berlage, H.P. et al.: *Arbeiderswoningen in Nederland* (Rotterdam 1921)

Bock, Manfred, Sigrid Johannisse and Vladimir Stissi: *Michel de Klerk, bouwmeester en tekenaar van de Amsterdamse School* (Rotterdam, year unknown)

Boeken, A: *Prijsvraag voor een gebouw voor de Rijksacademie van Beeldende Kunsten te Amsterdam* (Elsevier's Geïllustreerd Maandschrift, 1918, year 28, p. 439-443)

Boeyinga, B.T.: *Architect M. de Klerk* (Amsterdam 17 November 1964)

Boterenbrood, J.: *Plan Zuid* (Tijdschrift voor Volkshuisvesting, 15 May 1923, p. 146-154)

Boom, A.van der: *Moderne Bouwkunst in Nederland, het nieuwe Amsterdam* (Op De Hoogte, Christmas edition 1926, p.300-303)

Burkom, Frans van: *Michel de Klerk, bouw- en meubelkunstenaar 1884/1923* (Rotterdam 1990): *'Tintelend nieuw en nooit gezien', Michel de Klerks postkantoor aan het Spaarndammerplantsoen te Amsterdam* (Jong Holland 17, no. 3, 2001, p. 28- 43)

Casciato, Maristella: *The Amsterdam School* (Rotterdam 1996)

Casciato, Maristella and Wim de Wit: *Le case Eigen Haard di De Klerk 1913/21* (Rome 1984)

Dutilh, W.F.: *De wederwaardigheden van bewerkt mahoniehout* (1977)

Eigen Haard: *Maandblad van de woningbouwvereeniging Eigen Haard Amsterdam* (multiple volumes)

Fanelli, Giovanni: *Moderne architectuur in Nederland 1900-1940* (Florence 1968 / The Hague 1978)

Female resident: Droombeeld voor onze kinderen (Het Volk 28 November 1923)

Frank, Suzanne S.: Michel de Klerk 1884-1923, an architect of the Amsterdam School (New York 1970/ Michigan 1984)

Giedion, S: *Ruimte, tijd en bouwkunst* (1941, Dutch translation: 1954)

Gratama, Jan: *Beschouwing over de "Nieuwe Zakelijkheid"* (Moderne Bouwkunst in Nederland, no. 1, Rotterdam, p. 36-93): *Het werk van Berlage*

(volume Dr. H.P. Berlage en zijn werk, Rotterdam 1916, p. 24-51)

Hegemann, Werner: *'Aus der Amsterdamer Schreckenskammer'* (Wasmuths Monatshefte für Baukunst, No 4, 1925, p.147-151)

Heuvel, Wim J. van: *Renovatie in de Spaarndammerbuurt* (Polytechnisch Tijdschrift, no. 6, jrg. 33, June 1978, p. 302-315)

Hitchcock, H.R. jr.: *Modern architecture, romanticism and reintegration* (New York 1929)

Holst, Richard Roland: *Naar aanleiding van de portretten, getekend door den architect M. de Klerk* (1924, in Over Kunst en Kunstenaars, p. 93-98)

Hoste, Huib: *Architectuur, Bouwblokken III*, (De Telegraaf 12 June 1916): *Aan het Spaarndammerplantsoen* (De Telegraaf 8 June 1918)

Holzbauer, Wilhelm and Yukio Futagawa: *Michel de Klerk* (GA 56, 1980)

Jonker, Menno, Alice Roegholt and Floris Leeuwenberg: *De Amsterdamse School, verbeelde idealen* (Amsterdam 2011)

Judit, Tihani- Halmos György: *Az Amszterdami Iskola 1910-1930* (Budapest 1993)

Keppler, Arie: *Een kunstenaar, een edel mensch is heengegaan* (Tijdschrift voor Volkshuisvesting en Stedebouw, 15 December 1923, p. 321)

Klerk, Michel de: *De invloed van Dr. Berlage op de ontwikkeling der Nederlandsche bouwkunst* (Bouwkundig Weekblad, March 1916)

Kneppers, Marcel: *Het interieur van het postkantoor van Michel de Klerk gerestaureerd* (Amstelodamum, monthly magazine, year 90-2, March/April 2003, p. 19-29)

Kramer, Piet: *De Klerk* (Architectura 29 December 1923, p. 240): *De bouwwerken van M. de Klerk* (Wendingen, 1924, no. 9/10)

Kreis, Dr. W: *"Aus der Amsterdamer Schreckenskammer"* (Wasmuths Monatshefte für Baukunst, No 4, 1925, p. 210-211)

Kromhout, W.: *M. de Klerk* (Architectura, 29 December 1923, p. 230)

Mendelsohn, Erich: *Nagedachtenis M. de Klerk* (Berliner Tageblatt, December 1923)

Michael, Vincent L.: *Expressing the Modern, Barry Byrne in 1920s Europe* (Journal of the Society of Architectural Historians 69, nr. 4, December 2010, p. 534-555) *The Architecture of Barry Byrne* (Chicago)

Mieras, J.P.: *De Zuidkant van Amsterdam* (Bouwkundig Weekblad 1923, no. 22, p. 237-244): *Over het tekenwerk van M. de Klerk* (Wendingen, 1924, year 6, no. 2)

Mieras, J.P. and F.R Yerbury: *Dutch Architecture of the XXth Century* (London 1926)

Minnucci, Gaetano: *Moderna Architettura Olandese* (Architettura e Arti Decorative 1924, XI)

Molema, Jan: *Spangen en Spaarndammerbuurt, verschillen in volkswoningbouw* (Amstelodamum 2003, year book 95, p. 178 -214)

Moltzer, M. J.A.: *Nationale woningraad, In memoriam K.P.C. de Bazel en M. de Klerk* (in Tijdschrift voor Volkshuisvesting en Stedebouw, 15 December 1923, p. 348)

Olyslager, Hanneke: *Indische invloed op het werk van Michel de Klerk* (Jong Holland, year 4, no. 4, 1980, p. 21-31)

Ons Amsterdam: *Amsterdamse School* (Ons Amsterdam, October 1973, year 25, no. 10)

Oud, J.J.P: *Naar aanleiding van 'Arbeiderswoningen in Nederland'* (Tijdschrift voor Volkshuisvesting, 15-1-1922, p. 18-19)

Pasanea, E: *Amsterdamse School in dienst van de volkshuisvesting* (Amsterdam 2010)

Robertson, Howard: *Modern Dutch Architecture* (Architectural Review, August 1922, p. 46-50)

Roegholt, Richter: *Amsterdam in de 20e eeuw, deel 1, 1919/1945* (Utrecht/Antwerpen 1976)

Sevenhuijsen, Aug. M.J.: *Nieuwe Bouwkunst in Nederland* (Blaricum 1927)

Searing, Helen: *"Eigen Haard": Worker's Housing and the Amsterdam School* (Architectura 1971, no. 2, p.148-175)

Schiebroek, C.J.M. et al.: *Baksteen in Nederland, de taal van het metselwerk* (The Hague 1991)

Staal, J.F.: Bouwkunst, *M. de Klerk, bouwmeester 1884-1923* (Maandblad voor Beeldende Kunsten, 1926, year 3, p.178-185)

Stieber, Nancy: *Housing design and society in Amsterdam, reconfiguring urban order and identity, 1900-1920* (Chicago & Londen 1998)

Vriend, J.J.: *De Amsterdamse School* (Amsterdam 1970, published in various languages)

Wattjes, J.G.: *Woningbouw "De Dageraad" in Amsterdam-Zuid. Architecten wijlen M. de Klerk en P. Kramer* (Het Bouwbedrijf year 1, 1924. p. 252-255)

Wibaut, Floor: *Twee grooten, die gingen* (Het Volk 1 December 1923)

Wils, Jan: *In memoriam M. de Klerk, 1884-1923* (Elsevier's Geïllustreerd Maandschrift, year 34, part 67, 1924, p.75)

Wit, Wim de, et al.: *The Amsterdam School, Dutch Expressionist architecture, 1915-1930* (New York / London, 1983)

Wijdeveld, H. Th.: *In memoriam M. de Klerk* (in Nederlandsche Ambachts- en Nijverheidskunst 1922, Rotterdam 1923, p. XIII- XV and in Mijn Eerste Eeuw, 1985, p. 50-51)

Zilverberg-Boas, M.: *Van Joodse genealogie naar Amsterdamse architectuur* (Hakehilla, year 32, p. 26)

Zwiers, L. and J.P. Mieras: *Steenconstructies* (Handboek Burgerlijke Bouwkunde, 1916)

CREDITS

Publisher
Museum Het Schip, 2012

Text
Museum Het Schip

Translation
Esther van Gelder

Design
Rutger Vos
www.rutgervos.nl

Photography
Rutger Vos

Print
robstolk®
www.robstolk.nl

Illustration credits
Alice Roegholt (25, 64, 101l, 105a 106r, 138b)
Archief Ton Heijdra (31, 49, 50, 70, 77, 80, 92, 104, 127, 138a)
Isabel van Lent (143)
Rutger Vos (51a, 59, 65, 66b, 56r, 68, 72, 93r, 95a, 103r, 114a, 114lb, 137, 139a)
Han van Zwieten Architecten (128, 132)
F.R. Yerbury, Architectural Association School of Architecture (AA), London (56b, 69, 78, 119)
Nederlands Architectuur Instituut (NAi) (6, 20, 23, 42, 43, 51b, 57, 66a, 102, 105a, 106l, 108b, 120)
Stadsarchief Amsterdam (113, 114rb)
Archief Museum Het Schip (8, 10, 18, 19, 20, 21, 24, 30, 32, 33, 34, 35, 36, 44, 46, 47, 48, 56a, 58, 67l, 71, 79, 81, 82, 83, 84, 90, 91, 93l, 94, 95b, 100, 101r, 102l, 107, 108a, 114, 116, 117, 118, 126, 130, 131, 139b)

Contributors
Ton Heijdra, Alice Roegholt, Richelle Wansing, Erlynn Pasanea, Vladimir Stissi, Lieneke Poelman, Marije van Wijngaarden

Acknowledgements
Hildo Krop, Nederlands Architectuur instituut (NAi), Architectural Association School of Architecture (AA), Eigen Haard, Stadsdeel West, Vrienden Museum Het Schip en alle schenkers van fotomateriaal.

Museum Het Schip
Visitor address:
Spaarndammerplantsoen 140
1013 XT Amsterdam

Dependance De Dageraad
Visitor address:
Burgemeester Tellegenstraat 128
1073 KG Amsterdam

The book may be ordered through
Museum Het Schip
Oostzaanstraat 44
1013 WN, Amsterdam,
The Netherlands
Email: info@hetschip.nl
Phone + 31 (0) 20 4182885

www.hetschip.nl

This book was realised with the financial support of the Amsterdam Federation of Housing Corporations and Housing Corporation Eigen Haard.

ISBN/EAN: 978-90-814397-4-9